THE
QUARTERBACK
WHISPERER

THE
QUARTERBACK
WHISPERER

How to Build an Elite
NFL Quarterback

BRUCE ARIANS
AND LARS ANDERSON

hachette
BOOKS

NEW YORK   BOSTON

Hachette Books
Hachette Book Group
1290 Avenue of the Americas
New York, NY 10104
hachettebookgroup.com
twitter.com/hachettebooks

First Edition: July 2017

Hachette Books is a division of Hachette Book Group, Inc.

The Hachette Books name and logo are trademarks of Hachette Book Group, Inc.

The publisher is not responsible for websites (or their content) that are
not owned by the publisher.

The Hachette Speakers Bureau provides a wide range of authors for speaking events.
To find out more, go to www.hachettespeakersbureau.com or call (866) 376-6591.

Photo credits (page xi): (top left) B.A. and Peyton Manning © Associated Press;
(top right) B.A and Ben Roethlisberger © George Gojkovich / Contributor / Getty
Images; (bottom left) B.A. and Andrew Luck © MCT / Contributor / Getty Images;
(bottom right) B.A. and Carson Palmer © Associated Press

Print book interior design by Timothy Shaner, NightandDayDesign.biz

LCCN: 2017938896
ISBNs: 978-0-316-43226-9 (hardcover), 978-0-316-43225-2 (ebook)

Printed in the United States of America

LSC-C

10 9 8 7 6 5 4 3 2 1

To everyone I've looked up to in my life named Coach,
especially Charlie Robertson, John Devlin, and Jimmy Sharpe.
But more than anyone, this book is dedicated to
my first coach: My dad.

CONTENTS

THE
QUARTERBACK
WHISPERER

Peyton Manning with the Indianapolis Colts
Ben Roethlisberger of the Pittsburgh Steelers

Andrew Luck of the Indianapolis Colts
Carson Palmer of the Arizona Cardinals

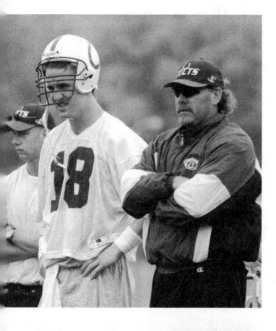
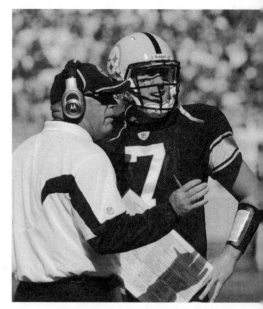

Bruce is a gambler at heart, and he's always thinking about how he can set up the defense to deliver that knockout punch. That's why quarterbacks love playing for him: He takes as many shots down the field as any coach in the NFL. And he never—never—plays scared.

— BEN ROETHLISBERGER

CHAPTER 1

THE PERFECT QB

I've always had a bit of a wild streak.

When I was five, living in the one-stoplight town of Marlowe, West Virginia, I would press my face close to the glow of the black-and-white TV screen and quickly be mesmerized by the *Adventures of Superman*. Every day, I closely studied his every move. I just *knew* I could be him—do what he did. So one summer afternoon I took my favorite red towel out of the bathroom closet, tied it around my neck, and climbed out my second-story bedroom window onto our porch roof.

My dad was then working as a mechanic at a garage across Highway 11 in front of our house. One of his coworkers saw me up on the roof and yelled, "Hey, Bert, is that your kid? I think he's about to jump!"

My dad sprinted across the road, pumping his legs like he was running a 100-yard dash. But I jumped, man, leaping into the sky with my arms outstretched, fully believing that I was going to take flight like Superman. Unfortunately, Newton's

laws applied to me just as they do to every human being. *Bam!*
I crashed onto the grass, lucky I didn't break my neck. My dad
reached me and quickly knelt down. "Are you okay, Bruce?"
he asked, hovering over me. "Are you okay, boy?"

"I can't fly, I can't fly!" I cried, more embarrassed than hurt.

When I was younger I wasn't allowed to drink milk,
because I was allergic to it. Was that going to stop me from
drinking something that was surely going to make my bones
stronger? Hell no. So I drank paint. Sure, I had to get my stomach pumped twice, but I had to try to put something down
my throat that looked like milk and might make me harder to
tackle when playing in our neighborhood football games.

At high school parties I'd rip the caps off beer bottles with
my teeth just to get wide-eyed looks from the girls. I could
be a little rough on the basketball court, sometimes playing
like I was in shoulder pads and a helmet. I got booted from a
game after I took out a player on the other team with a hard
foul. I thought he deserved it—he'd been lippy for about three
quarters—but the referee believed otherwise.

When I was seventeen I got kicked out of York Catholic
High School in York, Pennsylvania, after I was caught drinking beer with my football buddies during a school retreat. We
had a hell of a time that night out in the wilds of Maryland—a
suitcase full of booze made sure of that—but nothing was
worth the look of disappointment on my father's face when he
learned I was no longer welcome at my high school.

"One of the boys on the retreat got really drunk and broke
a bottle and cut himself really badly," says my wife, Chris, who
I started dating in high school. "Bruce went to find the priest to

say that the kid really needed help. All the boys got in trouble, but only Bruce got expelled. It turned out to be the best thing that ever happened to him. At this point, Bruce didn't have big dreams. He knew he didn't want to be a welder because he'd had a part-time job doing that and he didn't like it. But he wasn't driven to succeed. Getting kicked out of school gave him that drive. He wanted—needed—to prove everybody wrong."

Chris is right: I now had my mission in life. But this was a very difficult situation, especially for my dad. He was a working man; he ended up toiling on the factory lines at Caterpillar Inc. in York for more than twenty-five years, taking every overtime shift he could to support his wife and five kids. When my dad and I were told I had been dismissed from my school, I knew I had failed him. We thought all the scholarships I had worked so hard to earn were now going to be gone. Worse, I had brought shame to the name he had labored so hard to uplift and honor.

I've been haunted by that heartbreaking look he gave me back then. I've seen it in my mind at every stop of my coaching career. When the day finally came, in 2006, when I was a Super Bowl winner—I was the wide receivers coach for the Steelers—I remember so vividly looking up into the stands after we had defeated the Seahawks and spotting my dad. With confetti on my shoulders, I saw that the look of abject disappointment on my father's face of so many years earlier had finally turned into a portrait of joy and pride. Talk about the redemptive power of sports.

I bartended my way through college at Virginia Tech— sometimes I had to hustle from football practice to be on time for my shift—and I loved working late nights so I could listen to boozy old-timers share their stories. They all told me variations of a single theme, a lesson I carried with me long after I quit slinging cocktails. "In life," the old-timers said time and again, "you must take chances."

You do in football as well. During my senior season at Virginia Tech I was a wishbone quarterback, one with hair that fell below my shoulders and a mustache that would have made Jimmy Buffett jealous. I looked like a rebel. And I sure as hell tried to play like one.

If we had the ball at the one-yard line and the defensive backs were playing at the line of scrimmage in press coverage, our coach, Jimmy Sharpe, would tell me, "We're calling the 'Go' route." And sure enough, I was going to take my shot— even though we might have 99 yards to go for a score. You can't play or coach in fear, ever, and if there's one word that's not in my vocabulary it starts with the letters c-o-n-s-e-r and ends with v-a-t-i-v-e.

That's always been my coaching philosophy: *No risk it, no biscuit.* I've been calling plays for nearly forty years. I'll always give my quarterback at least two options based on how the defense lines up. One option will give us a chance to make a first down; the other option will give us a chance to score a touchdown, no matter where we are on the field. My quarterback must always have in the very forefront of his mind, *If I have the right matchup and the opportunity is there to take a shot at the deep ball, take it.* I don't care if it's third-and-three; if our best receiver is in single coverage and he's running a deep post route, throw him the goddamn ball.

Veteran NFL quarterbacks are often hesitant to do this. They want to take the easy completion. When I began working with Carson Palmer in Arizona in 2013 I told him, "Have fun. Throw it deep. This is what we do."

He looked at me like I had three eyes. "Really, B.A.?" he asked me. "I can look at the deep ball like that on virtually every play?"

"Hell yes," I replied. I wanted Carson to look down the field as often as he could. It was like he had a restrictor plate on him his entire career, and I was the coach who was going to pull it out of his engine and let him rev his arm at as many RPMs as possible. Of course, if the deep routes were covered, then I would want him to check down to a shorter throw.

With the young quarterbacks it's always been easier to teach this go-for-broke approach to offensive football. I remember telling Andrew Luck when he was a rookie with the Colts, "Andrew, this is easy. I don't care if it's third-and-one. If you got T. Y. Hilton matched up one-on-one, throw it to him. It's that simple."

Andrew smiled at me like he had just won the lottery. "I can do that?" he asked. "Really?"

"You bet, kid," I said. "Let 'er rip."

Andrew bought in right away to the old but true saw that you have to play smart, not scared. And playing smart means exploiting the matchups you have on the field, especially when it comes to launching the deep ball, which is always the most enjoyable thing to do on the football field.

One of my favorite play calls of all time came when I was the offensive coordinator for the Steelers and we were playing in the AFC Championship Game against the Jets in January 2010. We were leading 24–19 in the fourth quarter and facing a third-and-six at the Jets' 40-yard line when the scoreboard showed two minutes remaining in the fourth quarter.

Ben Roethlisberger came over to the sideline and we began talking. The Jets were out of timeouts. Right away I told him we were going for the kill shot; screw running the ball to take time off the clock. This is always the most important call of the game—the play that can get you a first down to end the game by taking kneeldowns.

I pulled Ben close. I told him that Rex Ryan, the Jets' head coach and defensive mastermind, was going to have his guys line up in their Bear defense with nine players close to the line of scrimmage. Rex had been doing that all year in this situation and I knew he wasn't about to change. Hell, his dad, Buddy, who invented the "46 defense," did the exact same thing when he was a defensive coordinator and head coach in the league. Like his father, Rex is an aggressive coach and he was going to do everything he could to stop the run and force us to punt.

I told Ben, "We're going for the fucking throat." Ben just flashed a sly little smile at me, a veteran's shit-eating grin. Right then I knew it was our ball game.

Ben approached the line of scrimmage. Sure enough, the Jets were in their Bear package—nine defenders so close to Ben he could practically feel the heat of their breath as he called out the signals. He took the snap and rolled the right. We had wide receiver Antonio Brown running from the left side of the field to the right. Ben fired a great pass for a 14-yard gain.

First down, kneeldown, ball game.

I can't stand it when coaches play not to lose, like when a head coach with a five-point lead will run the ball three straight times with two minutes to play and kick it and ask the defense to win him the game. That's not my way, brother. I'll never be too afraid to throw it and take the heat if it's incomplete. My job as an offensive coach is not to allow our defense to retake the field. Run out the clock and kneel down—that's my job.

And there is no feeling in football that is better than watching those final seconds tick off the clock and knowing the guy on the other sideline is utterly helpless to do anything about it. It's delicious, almost as satisfying as sex—*almost.*

I'll never forget the day I became a quarterback.

I was eight years old and playing on my local Pee Wee team. I began the season as our center. But one afternoon at practice after our first game, I intercepted a pass. Then I threw the ball to our coach. It was a perfect spiral, and the coach liked what he saw.

"You've got a nice arm, Bruce, so I'm going to make you our quarterback," he said to me. "You're smart enough to know what to do out there. You're running the show now."

Oh man, I loved being in charge—loved calling the plays in the huddle, loved taking the snap, loved chucking the ball around the field. It was so invigorating. I immediately knew that this was what I wanted to do with my life. Somehow, some way, I was determined to be a quarterback for as long as I could.

I played both quarterback and defensive back in high school, and I actually began my college career at Virginia Tech as a safety. But then one day at practice during my freshman year I intercepted a pass and threw the ball forty yards back to the head coach. He too liked what he saw. From that day forward I was a quarterback.

In my five seasons at Virginia Tech I had five different offensive coordinators who ran four different offenses. This exposed me to hundreds and hundreds of different plays. By the time I was an upperclassman I'd sit in meetings and a coach would see that I was lost in my own world. "Arians, are you on drugs?" the coach would ask.

"No sir," I'd say. "Just thinking about different plays."

And I was—always. Football was a giant chess game that I played in my head. I could think for hours about certain plays and how I could get them to work against any defense. Nothing in life other than my wife occupied my imagination like the strategy of football. The coaches saw my passion, and they let me call the offensive plays for our junior varsity team when I was a fourth-year junior.

Before my senior year, Jimmy Sharpe became the Hokies' head coach. I had no intention of playing for him. I interviewed at a junior high school in northern Virginia for a teaching and coaching position, but I didn't get the job. Who knows how my life would have turned out if I had done better in that interview? With no other really good options, I agreed to meet with Coach Sharpe.

I looked like hell. I had injured my ankle playing pickup basketball, so I limped into his office with a cane. My weight was up 225 pounds—I had played at 190 the previous year—and I had a grizzly blond beard. Coach Sharpe looked me up and down as I shuffled into his office and said, "You gotta be shitting me. I hope to God you're not my starting quarterback."

I laughed and told him that I just needed to get into shape. Then I spent three hours describing to him what changes needed to be made to turn the program into a winner. He was going to install a wishbone attack, and I had run the wishbone as our scout-team quarterback the previous fall as we prepared for Alabama (who beat us 77–6). I told him I could be his quarterback and I would help him win.

He knew that I bartended at Carlisle's and that a lot of the players hung out there. This gave me some status with my teammates, and Coach Sharpe figured if he could win me over then I could help him win the rest of the team over. He was a very smart cat.

Coach Sharpe and I quickly became attached at the hip. He treated me like an extra coach on the field. We talked plays and strategy and players at all hours. I only played for him for one year, but he became my mentor—someone I would trust for the rest of my life.

He let me coach the quarterbacks even as I was our starting quarterback. I just loved helping those young guys maximize their talent. And that was when I knew I had found my life's calling—I knew I wanted to become a quarterback whisperer.

What does the perfect NFL quarterback look like?

It begins with something you can't see. He must have heart—a big heart, a lion's heart, a heart that beats for an entire franchise. Heart is exhibited when a quarterback plays through pain, when he smashes into a 320-pound defensive lineman on third down to try to gain those extra six inches for the first down, or when he throws an interception and then runs forty yards down the field to make a tackle. Whenever a quarterback puts the team above himself, that's an expression of heart. If a quarterback doesn't have this, his teammates will see it—and he won't have a chance to make it in the league because his teammates won't believe in him. The quarterback doesn't have to be the most popular player in the locker room, but he sure better have the respect of every man on the roster. And that level of respect is possible—it's achievable—through displays of heart.

Another trait he must have is what I call "grit." This is the ability to handle success and failure equally. A quarterback has about twenty-five seconds from the moment he walks to the line of scrimmage and scans the defense to when the play is over. Dozens of decisions need to be made by the quarterback in those twenty-five seconds: Do I change the play based on how the defense is lined up? If so, what should I change it to? If the play is a pass, what receiver will be my hot receiver— the one that should be open—if there's a blitz? Is my offensive line in the right protection? Does my running back know where to pick up the potential blitzing linebacker? Are the defensive backs playing zone or man coverage? Are the safeties creeping toward the line of scrimmage or are they hanging back? Where is the most vulnerable spot in the defense that I can exploit? Where are the strongest spots in the defense that I need to avoid?

Then, in the average of about four seconds from the snap to the end-of-play whistle, so many things can go right or wrong for the quarterback. A called play in an NFL game only works about half the time. But what really matters is how the quarterback reacts to what transpires on each and every play. When a play doesn't go as designed, the quarterback must not sulk, lose his temper, or even convey a sense of frustration. And he sure better not let his grit waver. Still, I don't want him to completely wipe the play from his memory—he needs to learn from what he just experienced on the field—but he needs to quickly move on and be the leader of his offense. QBs must always—always—act like the next play is going to be a touchdown, even if they don't truly believe it. The quarterback needs to project calm and poise and steely-eyed confidence. This is grit, living play-to-play and growing play-to-play.

Another characteristic the NFL quarterback must have that you can't see is the ability to process a vast amount of information in a short amount of time and make prudent decisions based on that intelligence. Twenty years ago NFL defenses typically had ten different coverage formations and five different blitz packages. But now a quarterback will see that many in the first two series of a game. So the quarterback must have an agile, quick mind to read the defense, anticipate what is coming, and make the appropriate change at the line of scrimmage to exploit the defense at its most vulnerable area.

The time from when the ball is snapped to when it must come out of the quarterback's hand on a throw is usually less than three seconds. So the quarterback literally has to make dozens of rapid decisions—he has to read the defense, figure out where the most vulnerable area on the field will be, identify his hot receiver, make sure his protection is lined up correctly—that determine whether or not a play succeeds or fails. No other position in sports requires this much on-the-fly thinking. This is why quarterback is the hardest position to play in all of sports.

Another change in the game from two decades ago is that back then the same eleven defenders essentially stayed on the field for the entire game, unless they became injured. But now defenses will use twenty different players in a game, many of them specialists whose singular, ultimate job is to make life miserable play after play for the quarterback. This makes it infinitely more difficult for the quarterback to know at the snap of the ball which receiver will have an advantage and which defensive lineman is most likely to win his matchup against a certain offensive lineman in front of him. In other words, it's now more challenging and confusing than ever to play quarterback in the NFL.

So many quarterbacks who are drafted high fail—and that has nothing to do with their physical talent. It's what exists between their ears that matters most, that determines whether one will flourish or flounder in the NFL. Why don't some first-round draft picks last very long in the league? General managers fell in love with their ability to throw a ball down the field and are seduced by their potential.

But what is very hard to measure when you're scouting college quarterbacks is how they are going to react to the complexity of NFL defenses. This has nothing to do with arm strength and everything to do with mental strength. There's that fundamental thing again—grit. I can't overemphasize how important it is to have a fast, fertile mind to play quarterback in the NFL. And also how important it is to have the study habits of an Ivy League doctoral student. If a quarterback isn't willing to put in the work during the week then he'll have no chance at success on Sundays. Zilch. Zippo. We use every teaching tool: film, notes, field work, homework, and now virtual reality reps, which are priceless.

On the practice field I spend the most time with my quarterbacks reviewing what transpires during the three to four seconds of a basic pass play. First and foremost, the quarterback has to understand his protection, because the defense can always blitz one more guy than you can block. So at the line the quarterback has to read—predict—what he thinks the defense is going to do, and then understand where his hot receiver is going to be if a safety, a linebacker, or multiple defenders come on a blitz. Then once the ball is snapped, as the quarterback is dropping back—let's say he sees that no blitz is coming— what must he do? He needs to quickly analyze the coverage. Is it zone or man? Are the safeties in the middle of the field or on the edges? The quarterback has to go through his progressions of potential receivers—one, two, three, four, five. If the safeties split to the edges, the quarterback's progression is from inside out. If the safeties rotate inside to the middle of the field, his progression is just the opposite, outside in.

Then the ball has to come out of the quarterback's hand on time. We have plays that are called rhythm throws where the quarterback's back foot hits the end of his drop and— *whoosh!*—the ball flies out of his hand. Probably the hardest throw in football is the rhythm throw, because the ball must leave the quarterback's hand before his receiver makes the final cut on his route. We also have what we call hitch throws, where the quarterback hits the end of his drop, hitches up a step, sets his feet and—*bam!*—he flings the ball. Timing is everything in the NFL; if a quarterback doesn't have this skill—this one that *really* can't be taught—he won't last long in the league. An NFL QB either has this skill—this gift—or he doesn't. I'll take a quarterback with a great sense of timing any day over one with a big arm who struggles to make those rhythm throws.

The ideal quarterback also needs to be a leader. Virtually all of the great NFL quarterbacks have been extroverts, guys who love being around other guys and are life-of-the-party types. You can feel their presence when they walk into the room. There are exceptions, but most often the successful quarterback is a natural-born leader, a Patton in pads.

A leader is willing to take risk and pay the price. The opening lines from one of my favorite poems, "If—" by Rudyard Kipling, come to mind:

> *If you can keep your head when all about you*
> *Are losing theirs and blaming it on you;*
> *If you can trust yourself when all men doubt you,*
> *But make allowance for their doubting too;*
> *If you can wait and not be tired by waiting . . .*

What do these words mean to me? Simple: When the time comes to roll the dice—and that time comes for all of us— you'll succeed if you keep your wits and stay focused on the task at hand.

* * *

The most important physical attribute of the ideal quarterback is the ability to throw the ball with accuracy to all parts of the field. If a receiver is open by half a step, the quarterback needs to be able to hit him in stride on the short passes, the intermediate-length throws, and the deeps balls. It's very difficult to teach a quarterback to become accurate once he is in the NFL; this is a trait that leaps off the college film in the scouting process. Of course, you want your quarterback to have a strong arm, but it's much more important to be accurate with the ball. If a kid is missing easy throws in college, I'll think twice about drafting him or signing him as a college free agent. By the time a college QB is twenty-one or twenty-two he either has a well-developed sense of anticipation and accuracy or he doesn't. The cold truth is that NFL coaches can't develop those skills.

The final thing the ideal NFL quarterback needs—and this really is just the cherry on the top of the sundae—is athleticism. Now, I'm not talking about the need to be a great athlete. You look at past big-time college QBs who couldn't make it in the NFL. They were plenty athletic. But they couldn't process information at the NFL level and be accurate enough to play the game. In college they could make enough of the throws and then beat defenses with their legs. But you can't do that in the NFL; the defensive players are too big and fast. That's why the read option will never be a consistent staple in the pro game. If you put your quarterback in harm's way enough, after all, harm will come to him.

An athletic NFL quarterback simply needs to be able to move in and out of the pocket. You don't have to be fast.

Tom Brady and Peyton Manning would never be described as fleet-of-foot speedsters. But they can move a step or two and then be extremely accurate with their throws even if they aren't perfectly balanced. Ben Roethlisberger has never been the quickest guy, but he can roll out and complete a throw with defenders hanging all over him. Damn, that's athleticism.

So if you take everything I just described about the ideal NFL quarterback—the heart, the grit, the smarts, the ability to lead, to throw with accuracy, and to have just enough athleticism—who do you get? Who would qualify?

If I could draw the perfect quarterback, it would be a mixture of all the top guys I've coached: the heart and mind of Peyton Manning; the grit and leadership of Big Ben; the athleticism of Andrew Luck; and the arm of Carson Palmer.

The most important relationship a head coach has on his team isn't with the other coaches, the owner, or the general manager. It's with the quarterback. He's the one who runs the show on the field; he's the ultimate extension of his coach. If there isn't a high level of mutual trust between them, both coach and quarterback will be doomed.

That's why I've always treated my quarterbacks like family. I play golf with them, go to dinner with them, talk to them about their personal lives, their kids, wives, girlfriends, partners, and their aspirations and dreams for the future. These are the same kind of discussions I've had with my own kids, Jake and Kristi.

Sometimes quarterbacks see ghosts out there on the field. They think they spot a certain coverage when they really don't. So you have to have an open dialogue with them once they get to the sideline. I need to tell my quarterback that a defender is baiting him and tricking him, and my quarterback has to trust what I'm saying. The quarterback has to know that his coach isn't making crap up, that what I see is in fact correct and what he sees on the field is in fact incorrect.

To show my quarterbacks how much I believe in them, I let them pick their favorite plays that we'll run in the game. On the nights before a game we'll sit down in a hotel conference room and we'll have six third-down calls for certain distances. On third-and-five, for example, I'll ask my quarterback to give me his top three plays that he wants to run in that situation. Then on game day we'll do that. Not only does this give ownership of the game plan to my quarterback, but it also makes him more accountable for what happens during the game. I want my quarterback to feel like we are tethered at the hip—and at the heart.

I'll also ask my quarterback at our Friday meeting to give me his fifteen favorite pass plays. Then I'll get fifteen running plays from the coaches and I'll script the first thirty plays. If there is a pass play that I really want to include in those first thirty, I'll put it on the projector and make my case to the quarterback. But if he strongly disagrees, then I'll let him win that argument. Remember: Players make plays, not coaches. So it's vital that the quarterback be comfortable with the plays we will run. Because if he's not, no matter how much I'm in love with a certain play design, it won't work if my quarterback can't execute it.

We continue this dialogue during the game. I'm constantly asking my quarterback what plays he likes, what he thinks will work against the defensive looks we're seeing, and what calls he wants to avoid. These conversations are crucial to winning games.

But the fourth quarter is my time. This is when I generally tell my quarterback what plays we'll execute. Oh yeah, I'll still listen—hell, I'm always listening; that's probably the most important skill as a coach—but the fourth quarter is when I usually take charge. And when the pressure mounts as the game clock winds down, that's when I really like to go for the kill. Some offensive coaches sit on the ball in the fourth quarter. Not me, brother. This is often the best time to really cut it loose.

No matter the circumstance late in a game—if the game is tied or we're winning or losing—I always remind my quarterback of one thing: If the matchup is right, throw the ball deep. Don't hesitate, don't think twice. Don't ever waste an opportunity to crush the spirit of the defense by completing a long touchdown. And if it doesn't work, well, at least we didn't leave any damn bullets in the chamber.

My family moved from Marlowe, West Virginia, to York, Pennsylvania, when I was eight. As a kid I spent virtually all of my free time at Memorial Park, which was just down the street from my house on Springdale Avenue in our blue-collar neighborhood.

At the park we played every type of game—volleyball, tetherball, softball, baseball, basketball, and football. Some of the older guys at the park were African American, and I never thought twice about our different skin colors. One of the older black guys was named Eddie Berry. He played offensive line at York High and he gave me my first nick-name: S.Q. Smooth.

Esquire Smooth. I loved it. I carved it into the picnic tables at the park. Getting that nickname meant I was accepted at the park, and it did more for my confidence than anything else I ever did as a kid. I felt I belonged there, my home away from home. For us boys at the park, sports was our common lan-guage, our bond of brotherhood.

Another older kid who I admired at the park was Denny Stock, the starting quarterback at York High, who would even-tually earn a football scholarship to Lehigh. I studied Denny closely, how he carried himself, how he interacted with others, how he always seemed so composed and in control of every sit-uation. He had such an air about him, a confidence you could almost feel. He was cool personified to me—and my introduc-tion to what a quarterback should be.

Hut-hut-hut—HIKE!

These words were the soundtrack of my childhood, words that represented the wonderful promise of what could be accomplished on a football field. I soon became a quarterback myself, in both high school and college. For nearly fifty years, quarterbacking has been my life's work. Though I believe it is the most difficult position to play in all of sports, it can be mas-tered. In the thousands and thousands of hours I've spent on the field and in the film room I've learned a few secrets about quarterbacks—and how to turn potential into production.

Hut-hut-hut—HIKE!

Let's take the snap and break down the art of quarter-backing.

You really knew Bruce was bound to be an NFL head coach at some point. He had it in his blood.

— PEYTON MANNING

CHAPTER 2

PEYTON MANNING

It was December 12, 1999. The scene was the old RCA Dome in Indianapolis. The main character in this little tale: Peyton Manning, then in his second year with the Colts. I was his quarterback coach.

We were about to face the New England Patriots, a team that was clearly in Peyton's head. The previous fall, in just the second start of his rookie season, Peyton threw three interceptions in a 29–6 loss at Foxboro. Midway through the fourth quarter of the game, with the outcome already decided, Peyton was so frustrated that he asked for mercy: He wanted to be pulled from the game.

"Fuck no, get back in there," I told him. "We'll go no-huddle and maybe you'll learn something. You can never ask to come out. You're our leader. Act like it."

What happened after our talk was a sight to behold. Peyton led us on a late-fourth-quarter drive that culminated with a three-yard touchdown pass to wide receiver Torrance

Small—the only points we scored that day. We played fast and it seemed to give Peyton a shot of confidence. I filed those two distinctly different Mannings in my head.

Before that December 1999 game against the Patriots, I saw during pregame warm-ups that Peyton was a live wire of nervous energy, crackling with anxiety. He fidgeted like a Mexican jumping bean and he had a frowning, contorted face. Frankly, he looked like he really needed to go to the bathroom, even though he was all clear on that front.

I always study my quarterbacks during pregame warm-ups. I want to know if they're tense, uptight; if the ball is coming out of their hand nicely; if their drops are hurried; and whether they're in rhythm. You need them to stay in the moment—"the precious present," as basketball coach Rick Pitino describes it—and not look too far ahead. They just need to focus on what they can control and not worry about the game plan or the different defensive looks the other team is going to throw at us. Bottom line: Body language is so important to the quarterback position because the rest of the offense feeds off the quarterback. So if your quarterback looks shaky before a game, you need to do something about it—and damn fast.

Peyton kept fidgeting with his equipment. This was, in poker parlance, a classic tell, because I knew that whenever he adjusted and readjusted his left kneepad, he was really upset about something. Peyton can obsess with the best of them, and I knew he needed to be calmed down. I approached him on the field, determined to shift his focus.

"Peyton, your footwork is all messed up," I said. "What's wrong with you, man?"

Peyton then spent the final ten minutes of pregame perfecting his footwork, even though I saw that it had been flawless during his warm-up. I wanted him to quit worrying about the fact that we were about to play a team that had been his nemesis, his kryptonite. We'd lost three in a row to the Pats. And sure enough, Peyton's mind became so locked onto taking precise five- and seven-step drops that his anxiety vanished into the crisp December air.

I always want to know what's going on in the head of my quarterback. Is he happy? Sad? Mad? Stressed? Pissed? Calm? Irritated? A good quarterback coach is a part-time psychologist. You have to know the emotions of your most important player, because what's going on between his ears is just as critical as the physical part of the game.

After I got Peyton to focus on his footwork, it was as if his worries magically melted away. He was one smooth operator, brother. Playing cool, calm, and cerebral, he threw two touchdown passes and no interceptions in our 20–15 win over the Patriots, which was Peyton's first-ever victory over those guys. He would finish the season by earning his first invitation to the Pro Bowl.

But I think it was that pregame moment against the Patriots that was the turning point in my relationship with Peyton. I had pushed just the right psychological button. Recognizing and understanding nonverbal cues in others is essential to coaching at all levels, and I like to think I learned how to read people a long time ago in an unlikely place—behind a bar in Blacksburg, Virginia.

* * *

On Saturday afternoons during my fifth-year senior season at Virginia Tech, I called some of my own plays as the starting quarterback for the Hokies. We ran the wishbone, a formation that features a fullback and two halfbacks lined up behind the quarterback. My throwing stats weren't exactly Hall of Fame–worthy—I completed 53 of 118 passes for 952 yards with three touchdowns and seven interceptions—but I was a pretty good runner. I rushed for 243 yards and 11 touchdowns, still a school record. Not even Michael Vick when he played at Virginia Tech topped that TD mark!

But in what may have been a first in college football history, after the home games I dished out drinks from behind the bar at a restaurant named Carlisle's. I probably violated some NCAA rule, but I needed that dollar an hour and the free steaks.

I was familiar with the rhythms of the bartending world. Growing up in a blue-collar neighborhood in York, where my dad was a machinist and my mom worked on the line at the York Peppermint Pattie factory, I often visited a bar my grandfather worked at in Paterson, New Jersey. There, sipping on my nonalcoholic birch beer in the smoky haze, I observed and listened. You can learn a lot about human nature in a bar.

At Carlisle's I met all types of people—rich and poor, black and white, educated and high school dropouts. What I loved to do was just listen to people tell their stories. They'd open up to me about their life and times, their hopes and dreams and fears. I quickly realized that everyone has something valuable to say, from the janitor to the corporate executive, and if you're willing to just shut your mouth and listen you can learn so many valuable lessons from everyone you come across.

Listening is a dead art—especially in coaching, where too often people in charge just shoot off their mouths or rant and don't first ask questions of others and listen closely—but it's the only way to truly understand the narrative of people's lives, to know what they're feeling, to get what's important to them. I learned this at my grandfather's joint in Paterson, and I carried it with me when I attended Virginia Tech.

One Thursday night in Blacksburg I was bartending when virtually the entire team showed up at the bar. With my long blond hair and my big bushy mustache, I certainly looked more like a hippie student than a football player, which perhaps was why so many of the customers felt comfortable talking to me.

On this night the hours ticked by. Everyone was having a great time, and then suddenly a few coaches strolled through the door. Man, the players hauled ass out the back door; I don't know if I'd ever seen some of them move so fast, like their damn pants were on fire. The players weren't supposed to be there and I tried to cover for them. I saw one of the coaches and asked, "Hey, Coach, what are you doing here?"

"We heard all the players were in here drinking," he said.

"Nah," I replied.

"Well, what are you doing here?" the coach asked.

"Man, I'm just working," I said. "I need the money, Coach. Can I buy you a beer?"

I pushed a beer at him and it defused the situation, reinforcing what I had learned years earlier watching my grandfather: Free beer can often be the sweetest elixir.

* * *

Perhaps the most important thing I learned from behind the bar was how to measure people—a skill that would serve me well in coaching. It wouldn't take me long, just by looking into someone's eyes, to figure out a customer's emotional state. You always need to be hyperaware of your surroundings when you're bartending, and I think I developed a good sense of how to gauge situations and people's mental makeup simply by employing the powers of observation and listening. I didn't realize it at the time, but it was like I was getting an education that prepared me to handle the psychological side of being a quarterback coach. The skills I learned bartending—reading nonverbal cues, finding the right words to say to someone who looks downtrodden, grasping the power of listening— certainly helped me with Peyton.

In 1974, my fifth-year senior season, we finished 4–7 at Virginia Tech. I became the first in my family to earn a formal college degree. But I also earned my unofficial degree in coaching—although then I was never actually a coach.

During my first three years in Blacksburg I backed up future NFL QB Don Strock. I ran the scout team, because, frankly, I wasn't good enough to start. This meant every week I'd pretend to be the starting quarterback of the opposing team we were about to face. Some players hate being on the scout team, but I loved it. I let myself slip into the mind of the coaching staff we were about to play, analyzing why they did things certain ways, why one coach preferred one style of offense and other coaches used different ones. So I wasn't just mimicking their offenses; I was feeling them out, learning them, assessing what I personally liked and what I didn't. No, I wasn't formally a coach, but my coaching philosophy was slowly crystallizing.

After my final season of football in Blacksburg, I got a call from the Dallas Cowboys. A scout said they were interested in me. Then they sent me a letter and a pen. "We hope to sign you to your contract with this pen," the note said. I was thrilled. I proudly showed off the pen to Coach Sharpe, who had become my mentor.

"You do realize," Sharpe told me, "that the Cowboys have sent about a thousand of those pens to college seniors across the country."

Ah, I hadn't, but I tried to play it cool. "Of course," I said. "I'm not holding my breath or anything."

I knew I wasn't an NFL player. I was always honest with myself about my limitations as a quarterback. So after graduation, as I was still trying to figure out what I was going to do with my life, I became a graduate assistant coach on the Virginia Tech staff. The pay was minimal—and by minimal, I mean nothing—and Coach Sharpe allowed me to coach the quarterbacks, which was more responsibility than was given to virtually any other GA in the nation.

But I still needed more money to pay bills—even though my wife, Chris, was working at a bowling alley and pool hall while finishing her degree in biology—so I got another job on the side. I left Carlisle's to tend bar at a basement nightclub in Blacksburg.

One evening a man who I knew lived up in a cabin in the Blue Ridge Mountains sauntered in looking for trouble. He looked like he was straight out of the movie *Deliverance*. His long Rip Van Winkle–like beard may have been home to several different critters.

"Tonight," the man declared to me, "I'm going to drink and I'm going to fight."

"Well," I replied, "let's make the beer free for you, but go fight somewhere else."

A few hours passed. Then the man, filled with liquid fire, started pinching the posteriors of several different young women. I told him he had to leave.

The mountain man pulled out a black handgun and stuck it in my belly. "Throw me out now," he calmly said to me.

I was terrified. It's generally not good when an intoxicated man is pointing a gun at you. But just then the nightclub owner, wielding a blackjack, clubbed the man over the head, knocking him out cold.

"I never miss," the nightclub owner said to me, smiling wide.

"Well, the damn gun wasn't pointed at your stomach!" I replied.

That was my last night of bartending. I realized, when that gun was jammed in my gut, that perhaps coaching would be a better career path. My beautiful wife agreed.

Chris was my compass, my true north. Without her, I wouldn't even have lasted a year in college. We met our freshman year of high school. We had homeroom class together and I sat a few rows over from her. I couldn't take my eyes off her—or her nice butt. The next year she was in a French class that I had already taken. I volunteered to help her with her homework. She agreed—and man, I've loved the French ever since.

"Bruce sat three rows in front of me in our homeroom class when I first noticed him," Chris says. "He was real quiet. I mean, really quiet. He was tall and gawky. But then he started helping me with my French homework. Or at least he pretended to help me, because it gave him an excuse to talk to me. We started dating but it wasn't anything exclusive until our junior year. But then things got pretty hot and heavy. My family loved him."

I grew close to Chris's father, Robert Allen. He had earned a college degree in chemistry from Mount St. Mary's and he taught me the value of education. Before I met him, I'd never even thought about college. I came from a family of factory workers and all the Arians men simply went to work once they finished high school. That was the way of our world. I didn't know a thing about college until I met Robert. We'd play chess deep into the night—he taught me how to play and I'd only have a shot at beating him if he was on his third whiskey—and he'd spend hours talking to me about the value of higher education. Suddenly I began to look beyond my hometown for my future. My dreams expanded.

There were times in high school when my own father couldn't make it to my football games because he had to work late. But Robert Allen would always be there. And when I'd look up into the stands and see him, it was the ultimate motivation for me. I always wanted to impress him, because I knew winning his approval was a key to capturing Chris's heart.

Chris would often be seated next to him at the games, and man, she was a vision. She had short, dirty blonde hair and a smile that could stop traffic. She was five feet tall if you stretched her—and brother, that was five feet of fire—and her presence could fill up a room. Even back then, I knew not to argue with her. She was the smartest girl in her class and she always got in the last word. No surprise that years later she would become a lawyer after earning her JD from Temple.

When I went away to Virginia Tech, Chris enrolled at York College. I missed her dearly. So on Fridays after class, with two bucks in my pocket, I'd hitchhike to York—345 miles away—to spend two blissful days with her. Then on Sunday afternoons I'd hitchhike back to Blacksburg.

My GPA after my first semester without Chris wasn't exactly stellar: 1.6. I was on the fast track to flunking out. In the spring semester of my freshman year I decided enough was enough. I walked to a pay phone and dialed Chris's number. "I can't do this anymore," I told her. "I just can't do this anymore."

On the other end of the line I heard her scream, *"What do you mean? What do you mean you can't do this anymore?"*

"No, babe, I can't stand being here without you," I explained, ever so urgently. "So I guess we're going to have to get married."

"So that's your proposal?" Chris asked.

"Yes," I said.

"Oh my gosh." Chris gulped. "Then, well, okay!"

We were married three months later at St. Rose of Lima Church on Market Street in York. Our reception was at the

Tremont Restaurant, where Chris's grandmother used to cook meatloaf and pot pies. Later that night we hopped in her ten-year-old Buick Special and drove halfway to Blacksburg. We spent the night at a little roadside hotel in Staunton, Virginia. That was our honeymoon.

The next morning we rolled into Blacksburg around 8 a.m. That night at midnight I started a job at a steel mill in Roanoke. The rest of our lives took off happily from there.

We never asked our parents for anything—not money, not cars, not help with housing. We were incredibly young, but Chris and I believed that it was up to us to make our own way in the world, chart our own course. Heck, we didn't even ask our parents for advice. Our problems were our own, not theirs, and it was up to us to solve them. One of the most satisfying things I've ever read was a letter that Chris's dad sent to her shortly after we were married and living in Blacksburg. He wrote, "I don't worry about you because I know Bruce will never quit."

I still haven't quit—and I never will as long as I have air in my lungs and strength in my muscles.

"There's always been a lot of yin and yang to our relationship," Chris says. "Bruce is the social one and I'm more capable of solitude and just being alone. I feel like in our relationship one person's weakness is balanced by the other person's strength. And Bruce has always really valued me. Even when he's being a total idiot, I know he values and cares for me. That's why we work. And Bruce really is an affectionate guy. That's part of his appeal to so many of his players throughout the years. He makes you feel good about yourself so you like being with him. He's always searching for perfection, but if he sees you're trying your best, he'll tell you how much he appreciates what you're doing and how much that means to him. Hell, he's really just a big softie."

In 1975, my first season as a graduate assistant, our defensive coordinator at Virginia Tech was Charley Pell, who two years later would become the head coach at Clemson and then later at Florida. Charley was a defensive mastermind—he excelled at the Xs and Os of coaching—and many nights he'd see me as I was walking out of the office.

"Where do you think you're going?" Charley would ask.

"Home, Coach," I'd say. "I got my work done."

"Oh no you don't," he'd say. "Come in here and sit down."

Then for several hours Charley would make me pretend that I was the starting quarterback for the team we would face on Saturday. He wanted to know how I planned to beat our Virginia Tech defense.

I remember one time we were playing Wake Forest in three days and I told Charley that if I'm calling the plays for the Demon Deacons, I'm going to run a weak-side zone running play because on film I'd seen our outside linebacker consistently step the wrong way when this play would come at him. And sure enough, when we faced Wake seventy-two hours later, the Demon Deacons offensive staff must have called that play twenty times during the game. But Charley and our defense were prepared. We beat Wake Forest 40–10.

So almost every night as a graduate assistant, I matched wits against one of the best defensive coaches in the nation.

I loved that back-and-forth with Charley—it was an engaging intellectual chess match. For hours we would talk strategy and how a defense could beat certain offenses. For a budding offensive coach, this was truly my graduate-level work.

I got to know Peyton Manning when he was a high school junior and I was the offensive coordinator at Mississippi State. His father, Archie, had been a legendary quarterback at Ole Miss, and it didn't take a recruiting genius to understand there was no way Peyton would ever come and play for us at Mississippi State, the sworn rival of the Ole Miss Rebels. But I was in charge of recruiting quarterbacks and so I called Archie one afternoon and asked, "Hey, is there any way Peyton would consider coming to play for us?"

Archie laughed so hard he must have doubled over. No, Archie told me in his southern, sugar-polite way, Peyton would not be attending Mississippi State.

But I already knew all about this young Peyton Manning kid. I always wanted to know where the next generation of quarterbacks would come from, so I identified many and studied everything I could about one of them in particular—Peyton.

As boys, Peyton and his older brother Cooper were regulars in the training room of the New Orleans Saints, where Archie played quarterback from 1971 to 1982. One time, Cooper, the family comedian and a natural smooth talker, convinced one of the trainers to tape him up as if he were a member of the team. The trainer wrapped his ankles and wrists in tape. When Peyton saw his brother getting worked on, he asked to be taped up as well. A tradition was then born.

Before many practices, the two boys would run through the locker room looking like miniature versions of their dad with their ankles and wrists mummified in tape. And after practice they would jump in the whirlpool or sauna—just like players.

Why was this important? Because Peyton was learning the culture of football and the sacrifices it took to make it to the NFL.

After Saints home games little Cooper and Peyton would wait for their dad outside the locker room. They'd see Archie emerge, walking gingerly, so sore it was hard for him to move. He would always give a big hug to his lovely wife, Olivia, then his kids, and then he'd interact with fans, signing every piece of paper thrust at him. Peyton sometimes said, "Dad, let's go home," but Archie would just smile at his son and tell him to put a grin on his face. Years later Peyton would realize that out there with the fans, his dad was playing the role of the starting quarterback, remaining upbeat and patient even in the face of soul-crushing defeats week after week.

In my research and by talking with Archie, I learned that Cooper loved to show off the football skills of little brother Peyton. When Peyton was three he could take a snap from center and perform a five-step drop, which he proudly demonstrated to Cooper's friends. Peyton could also execute a seven-step drop. He'd bring a Nerf football up close to his ear, just like his dad did, run seven steps back, and then throw that squishy, almost-as-light-as-air thing with amazing distance and accuracy across the living room.

But maybe what was most surprising during Peyton's early years, in terms of his future in the NFL, was that as an eight-year-old he'd crawl onto Archie's lap and watch game film. Peyton would grow wide-eyed at the action, hypnotized. He soon began firing questions, machine-gun-like, about the game of football, about what his dad was looking at, why different players lined up in different spots on the field. It wasn't long before he badgered Archie incessantly: "Daddy, daddy, can we watch film?" So began Peyton's utter obsession with watching film.

When Peyton was a teenager, he'd come home from school and begin reviewing tape of his own play, of other quarterbacks, and, if he could find it, of upcoming opponents. Concerned about his son's football single-mindedness, Archie would implore him to enjoy his teenage years. "Get a girlfriend," he said. "Go to a movie. You need to get out more."

Peyton's reply was always the same. "Daddy," he would say, "I've got to watch more film."

When Peyton started studying game film, Archie had just one request: "If you're going to watch film, do it the right way," he said. By that he meant, *Don't watch the ball, watch the defense; fans watch the ball.* To Peyton, every snap was like viewing a gripping blockbuster movie, full of nuance, mini-plotlines, and layers of complexity. After practice, after games, during the weekends, he'd watch tape of his own games, opponents' games, and NFL games. By the time he started high school, he knew more about defenses than some rookie NFL quarterbacks.

Archie didn't share much football advice with Peyton— he always wanted to be a dad first and foremost; he left the coaching to Peyton's coaches—but he did offer him one lesson in high school that Archie had learned the hard way. "You've got to know what you're doing out there because then you can get rid of the ball," Archie said, "and when you get rid of the ball you don't get hit." This nugget of wisdom further fueled Peyton's obsession with preparation.

I knew that Peyton was a highly competitive kid— he believed he would never lose and his temper would flare when he did, which was a good thing from my perspective. When Peyton was eleven his youth basketball team lost for the first time. Archie had been in the stands, as usual, watching intently. After the game the volunteer coach spoke to his players. "The reason you lost," he said, "was that you didn't have your minds ready to play."

Without missing a beat, Peyton piped up. Even then, he couldn't hold his tongue. "The reason we lost," the eleven-year-old declared, "is that you don't know what you are doing."

Archie, who'd been standing out of earshot, saw that Peyton and his coach had exchanged some heated words. On the car ride home he asked Peyton what he had said to his coach. As soon as Peyton told him, Archie pulled a U-turn, and minutes later Peyton was standing alone on the front porch of the coach's house. He rang the doorbell and, in tears, apologized.

Archie constantly told his boys the importance of respecting authority. He wanted them to be independent thinkers— especially when they were on the field of play and were forced to improvise, which was Archie's hallmark athletic skill— but they also needed to understand that their coach was ultimately in charge. Peyton was always respectful to me, even though I loved the fact that his temper could flare. You want a quarterback with fire in his eyes and in his belly, and Peyton certainly had both. That fire was the wellspring of his competitiveness.

When Peyton was a teenager, he came upon old films of Archie's college games. He asked Archie to put them in the TV. He watched Archie dart around linemen, outrun linebackers down the sideline, scramble in the backfield for what seemed like minutes at a time. At one point he turned to Archie. "Why aren't I fast like that?" he asked.

"I don't know, but it might be a blessing," Archie said. The father knew his sons would have to play the game differently than he did. Quarterbacks weren't relying on their legs as much anymore. They played with multiple wide receivers and they stayed in the pocket more now. Archie also insisted that throwing the ball down the field was the best way for an inferior team to beat a superior one, because if a throwing quarterback was special, he could carry the other ten players on his offense much easier than could a running quarterback. I couldn't have said that any better myself.

Peyton also learned from his dad that it was important to acknowledge the work of his offensive linemen. When Archie was in Houston he took his O-line to dinner one evening at Ruth's Chris Steak House and ran up a tab of over $1,000. When Peyton was in high school he wanted to pay for lunch for his offensive linemen, but sophomores like Peyton weren't allowed to leave campus. So instead he bought a pair of Isotoner gloves for each of them. Geez, just think about that: Peyton wasn't old enough to legally drive a car—he wouldn't be sixteen until the spring of his high school sophomore year—but he already had a keen understanding of how offensive linemen should be treated.

Peyton learned at a young age to avoid four common fundamental mistakes that young quarterbacks frequently commit: Never look behind you when you make your drop in the pocket; don't stutter-step after receiving the snap; don't pat the ball before you throw, because it will disrupt your timing with the receiver; and be perfectly balanced when you take the snap. Archie preached that like Old Testament truths to his sons.

As I watched high school tape of Peyton, I was stunned to see that by the time he was a senior he already had a pre-snap routine. After calling the play in the huddle, he would walk to the line of scrimmage. Before putting his hands under center, he would look at how the defense was lined up, his eyes darting from one side of the field to the other, then back, then back again. Then, on the film of his memory, he would quickly replay all of the tape he had watched of that opposing defense, trying to recall when he had seen this particular alignment. Once he pulled up the alignment from his mental catalog, he would remember what the defenders had done once the ball was snapped. Based on that, he had a good idea of where the defenders were about to move once the ball touched his hands. Now that's an accomplished QB—and Peyton was barely shaving once a week!

In the film room at Tennessee, where Peyton went to college, he filled up notebook after notebook with the details of offensive coordinator David Cutcliffe's offense. The strategy of football always fired Peyton's imagination, which was really the bedrock of all his success—and why NFL scouts fell in love with his play as far back as his freshman season in Knoxville.

The Volunteer coaches called Peyton "the Computer" and "R2D2" because of the way he studied. I also learned that Peyton would call out Cutcliffe when he believed he had made a mistake. If Cutcliffe told his quarterbacks to do one thing on a certain play, Peyton would check his notes to make sure that he had given the same instructions for that particular play weeks earlier. When Cutcliffe contradicted himself, his freshman signal caller would raise his hand and tell his coach that he was either making a mistake now or had committed a blunder weeks earlier. Peyton just wanted to know what his coach really intended on every play. Talk about preparation, preciseness, and mutual trust, for godsakes.

The Colts held the top pick in the 1998 draft. In our war room we debated selecting two players: Peyton or quarterback Ryan Leaf of Washington State.

I researched the hell out of both guys. The first time our group of decision makers met with Peyton was at the NFL Combine in Indianapolis. Four of us—general manager Bill Polian, coach Jim Mora, offensive coordinator Tom Moore, and myself—were sitting in a hotel room on the first floor of the Crowne Plaza when Peyton opened the door. Almost immediately, I could sense he had that "it" factor you're looking for in a quarterback.

He commanded the room; it was as if his presence just filled up every nook and cranny of the space. I asked him one question—I think it was about what style of offense he wanted to play in the NFL—and then he took over the interview, totally dominating the scene. We didn't ask another question. He fired queries, rat-a-tat-tat, at *us*. He wanted to know everything about our offense and how we planned to evolve it in the coming seasons. He asked about the receivers on the roster— he wanted to know their strengths and weaknesses—and who we planned to draft to upgrade the position. He asked about the running backs, the tight ends, the offensive linemen, even the defense. It was clear he had had a coach's mind. It almost felt like *we* were under the bright lamp and Peyton was an FBI investigator interrogating us.

The next night we had a meeting scheduled with Ryan Leaf. The four of us were back in the same hotel room. We waited. And waited. And waited.

Ryan Leaf didn't show. The dude blew us off.

We could see the difference between Peyton and Ryan even when the two were just getting measured and weighed at the Combine. When strength coaches finished poking and prodding Peyton, he asked how his body fat compared to other quarterbacks. He then reminded the coaches that one of his knees was swollen. I loved that: Peyton was competitive even about his body fat. Everything in life, to him, was a contest that he had to win.

Then Ryan Leaf stepped onto the scale at the Combine. He looked like crap; he was twenty pounds overweight. Yet Ryan, with the camera flashes popping in his face, proceeded to flex his biceps as though he was some goddamn Mr. America. It wasn't a good look.

Then the number on the digital scale popped up: 261. So

it was clear that Ryan hadn't prepared for the Combine, even though he should have viewed it as one of the most important events, and opportunities, of his life. I've got to trust my quarterback. Shit, my livelihood and the livelihoods of the entire coaching staff are in the hands of the quarterback that you select with the top overall pick. Face it, if you whiff on that player, you won't be employed for long. Ryan couldn't have made a worse first impression.

But we tried to keep an open mind after the Combine. Bill Polian loved Ryan's physical skill. He could make every throw and he reminded Polian of a young Jim Kelly with the toughness he had displayed at Washington State, leading the Huskies to the Rose Bowl that January.

We then held individual workouts with the two quarterbacks, starting with Peyton in Knoxville at the University of Tennessee campus. Peyton brought one receiver out to the field and he would have thrown for us all day—just throw after throw after throw. He grunted like a tennis player after each pass, and Bill thought he was straining. But I told Bill, "Hey, it's just one of those things that some quarterbacks do."

That evening I did my own detective work, like I always do when scouting a quarterback. I acted like I was a Tennessee alum and asked a softball player about Peyton; she had nothing but great things to say. I quizzed a secretary in the athletic department and an offensive lineman on the team. Both backed up the softball player, telling me that Peyton was a down-to-earth, rock-solid guy.

The next day we flew to Pullman, Washington, to work out Ryan. It was important for us to immediately spend time with him after we'd been with Peyton, because we wanted to compare the two back-to-back to maximize the validity of our memories and notes.

When we arrived, Washington State coach Mike Price had scheduled a workout on the stadium field for all his players who were hoping to play in the NFL. He also invited other NFL teams, so it wasn't really a private workout and we didn't get the one-on-one comparison we wanted.

Ryan then walked out onto the field and started going through a scripted workout that he had been preparing for. I went over to Coach Price and told him, "Look, we want him to throw the types of passes that we're going to ask him to make, not just the ones in the script."

"I don't think he'll do that," Mike told me.

"Well, he ain't getting drafted by us if he doesn't," I said. "We came here to see specific throws."

Eventually Ryan agreed to let us take over the workout, but we shouldn't have had to ask multiple times in the first place. It seemed like nothing was easy with him. But when he started making the throws we asked of him, man, did he ever light it up. What an arm. There wasn't a single throw he couldn't make. He had power, accuracy, and, when he needed it, a feathery touch. To me, his throws were artwork to be admired.

Then I became a detective again. I walked around Pullman the following day and talked equipment managers, janitors, and members of the women's volleyball team. No one had a nice thing to say about Ryan. I stopped at a 7-Eleven and spoke to the clerk behind the counter. He told me that Ryan had been banned from the store because of his boorish behavior.

I wrote up a report for the staff. You couldn't deny that he was 6'5", 250 pounds (on a good day), and could move and had a big, powerful arm. But there were so many red flags about his character and leadership ability. Peyton, conversely, didn't have as strong an arm as Ryan, but he was a natural-born leader who just couldn't get enough football. It was his oxygen, the sun in his solar system. I wrote that he was the type of young man you wanted leading your franchise.

Back at Indy, GM Bill Polian and Jim Irsay, the owner of the Colts, interviewed Peyton again. They asked him if he would be willing to come to mini-camp shortly after the draft if we selected him. "Oh, I'll be there," Peyton said. "Of course I'll be there."

They asked the same question to Ryan when they interviewed him. His answer was a little different. "Oh, I can't be there for that," he said. "I've got a deal set up during that time that I have to attend."

Still, there were people in our scouting department who really wanted to draft Ryan. I argued vigorously for Peyton. Two days before the draft, Bill called a meeting and informed us of his decision. He told us, "Peyton is our guy."

Peyton said the perfect thing to me right after we drafted him. "I'm ready to get to work," he said. "I mean, like right now."

We had those old Beta video machines and I immediately shipped mine down to New Orleans, where Peyton was staying. I sent him video clips of all our plays along with our playbook. He received the shipment on a Thursday.

I flew to New Orleans that Friday. The Beta machine was in his bedroom. I couldn't believe it, but Peyton already had a pretty high level of familiarity with our offense. He must have stayed up all night Thursday studying. We spent all day Friday in his room. I couldn't give him enough information.

A few weeks later, at our mini-camp for rookies and veterans, Peyton immediately took charge. We put the Beta machine in his hotel room, and the night before camp began we met from 6 p.m. until 2 a.m. going over plays. Six hours later Peyton stepped into the huddle on the first play and called, "Dice right, scat right, 92 X." The veterans just looked at him in astonishment. He seemed to know the whole damn playbook!

For the rest of camp Peyton rattled off play after play in the huddle like he'd been running the offense for a decade. The older players quickly realized that we had a very special guy under center.

But it wasn't just his mind that was impressive. If the defense was on the field and the offense was off on the side, he'd grab a few veteran receivers and tight ends and head to another field to throw. Peyton just wore them out. Marvin Harrison, Marcus Pollard, and Ken Dilger would be running up and down the field while Peyton uncorked pass after pass. I'd never seen a rookie quarterback win over a team so fast. And it wasn't anything that Peyton said; it was all in his actions and the fact that he was so prepared.

Peyton had been in an NFL locker room since he was five years old, literally the majority of his life. Nothing fazed him. He had been watching how an NFL quarterback with great character—his dad—interacted with his teammates, how he ribbed them if it was appropriate, or put his arm around a teammate if he was feeling down. Peyton instinctively knew how to act, even though he was only a rookie. I'd argue that no rookie quarterback in the history of the NFL was more prepared to walk into the locker room than Peyton. The other young guys would come into the locker room and you could see the fear in their faces; they were like, *Oh shit, what the hell do I do now?* But not Peyton; he was as cool and composed as any young person I've come across.

But of all the quarterbacks I've ever coached, Peyton was the most taxing on me. If we had a one-hour meeting, I needed to prepare three hours of material. He picked up concepts and plays and defensive tendencies so fast. I started calling him "the Piranha" because he devoured information. I had never seen—and haven't seen since—anything like that in a quarterback.

When Peyton moved from the Big Easy to Indianapolis he installed a projector with a Beta deck in his apartment. There were times I worried about him, because he spent hour after hour watching film. I mean, he had no social life. He watched every play from every practice, usually multiple times. Peyton was so obsessive that he even watched how to perform quarterback kneeldowns at the end of games. No detail was too minute. He put everything about football under the microscope. He needed to be the master of mastery.

But when it came to his personal life, well, Peyton needed a little help. I found out that he once arrived for a date with his future wife, Ashley, decked out head to toe in denim— and thought he looked ready for the red carpet. Another evening, as Peyton spoke to Ashley over the phone when he was at Tennessee and she was at the University of Virginia, he said that he was in the mood for Chinese food and was going to have it delivered. After he hung up Peyton then fumbled around trying to figure out how to place an order. He finally gave up, called Ashley back, and convinced her to phone a Chinese restaurant in Knoxville and order dinner for him.

In Indianapolis he was infamous for not being able to properly use a can opener. One time I visited him at his place and saw that he had pictures that his mom had given him on a closet door, showing what shirts went with what pants and shoes; she had picked out his outfits as if he was still in grade school. He kind of struggled with the basics of life, and it was a source of great comedy for his coaches and teammates. But he took all the jokes in stride. One thing and one thing only was important to him when he arrived in Indy: to become a great NFL quarterback.

That's what made it so easy to establish trust with Peyton— everything mattered so much to him. He was a football junkie and he loved working on his fundamentals of footwork and balance and arm position.

The first thing we really stressed with Peyton as a rookie was improving his arm strength. The only way to do that is to just throw and throw and throw, like a baseball pitcher does. So every day we would have him run a bootleg from about the 20-yard line, drop back to about the 30, have him set his feet, and then throw the ball as high as he could into the kicking net behind the goalpost. Peyton was dogged about this. And in every practice we could see his arm getting stronger. The release point of his passes got higher and the ball would end up higher and higher in the net. Mechanics were as important to him as his assignment on every play. And his footwork improved just as steadily as his arm strength.

I always looked at Peyton's arm angle as he released the ball. If a quarterback starts throwing it sideways, the ball is going to curve when it comes out of his hand and it will put a lot of pressure on the elbow. The ideal quarterback has the light feet of a boxer, the flexible hips of a golfer, and the powerful shoulders of a tennis player. You want your quarterback to reach up and throw down. Johnny Unitas did this better than anyone, but Peyton wasn't too far behind.

We also worked on how to hold the ball when making his drop. I wanted Peyton to have the ball close to his right ear as he set up in the pocket. Really, a quarterback can have it anywhere from the number to the ear; it's up to him to find out what's most comfortable. For Peyton, it was having the ball close to his ear.

I also stressed that his right leg needed to be positioned at what I call a "power angle," which is a 45-degree angle, as he prepared to throw—the velocity of passes always begins in the legs. The left foot should be framing the precise spot at which he was aiming down the field. After release, his belt buckle should be pointing directly at his target. These are fundamentals that every quarterback should strive to master.

The first year with Peyton was challenging for us; we ended up 3–13. I knew we were going to have trouble as early as the preseason when we struggled against . . . Ryan Leaf and the San Diego Chargers, who had selected Ryan with the second overall pick in the 1998 draft. Peyton threw two interceptions and Ryan carved us up, completing 15 of 24 passes for 172 yards. The Chargers won 33–3. But I was already hearing through the coaching grapevine—and trust me, the NFL is a very small world; there are very few secrets among coaches—that Ryan was a complete ass and had zero respect in the locker room.

The scuttlebutt proved accurate: Five weeks into the season, as Ryan and San Diego were preparing to come to Indy for a game, he had already cursed out a cameraman, launched into a profanity-laced tirade against a reporter, and been booed by his own home crowd. Man, if you lose your own fans only weeks into your NFL career, then you don't have a damn shot at winning over your locker room as a quarterback. I knew then, only a few games into Ryan's professional career, that the kid wouldn't last long in the NFL.

I stress again: So much of being an NFL quarterback has nothing to do with arm strength and being 6'5" and 250 pounds; at its core, it's about being a leader of men. Ryan just wasn't mature enough to handle either the day-after-day role or the inevitable adversity that every NFL quarterback will face. He only lasted four years in the NFL and later was sentenced to five years in prison after pleading guilty to felony burglary and drug possession charges in Montana. Sadly, Ryan became a cautionary tale. But I'm happy that Ryan is doing well today with the help of the NFL Legends program.

You could see in Ryan's and Peyton's rookie year that they were on completely different career paths. It was particularly sweet that the first win of Peyton's career came against

Ryan in our Week Five matchup with the Chargers. Peyton's stat line wasn't great—he was 12 for 23 for 137 yards and one touchdown—but he managed the game and guided us to a 17–12 victory.

Even though Peyton set five rookie NFL records in 1998, including most touchdown passes (26), he also threw a league-high 28 interceptions. But he hardly ever lost his confidence. I constantly reminded him that we had a rookie right guard, rookie receivers, and a tight end (Marcus Pollard) learning how to play the position after playing basketball in college. I said to him, "Hey, we're going to get better every week. Every week we're going to see a little improvement. It may not show up on the scoreboard, but we're getting better."

The only time I saw his confidence waver during his rookie season was at New England in an early-season game. He had just thrown his third interception when he came over to the sideline. Patriot cornerback Ty Law had baited him into throwing it—Law acted like he didn't know what pass pattern our receiver was running but in fact did—and picked him off. Peyton wanted to be benched. I told him, "You're not coming out. Let's go no-huddle and see if we can learn something in this last quarter to help us out."

Well, Peyton started slinging the ball all over the field. On the very first drive of going no-huddle in our two-minute offense we scored our only touchdown of the game. You could see—throw by throw, play by play—Peyton becoming more comfortable running an NFL offense. Everything began clicking with him. That's one of the most gratifying aspects of coaching, seeing a player learn on the fly and have the game

slow down for him. All the work he had put in as a player—
and I had put in as coach—was paying off. I knew right then
that he was going to become a great player.

Before his second year Peyton worked really hard at perfecting his play-action fake handoff during the offseason. I had
a bunch of film of Steve DeBerg when he was playing quarterback for the Chiefs in the 1980s, and I thought he was one
of the best play-action quarterbacks I'd ever seen. So Peyton
and our backup quarterback Kelly Holcomb watched hours of
DeBerg and his play-action fakes. Then they made a game out
of practicing their fakes out on the practice field, challenging
each other to see who could pull off the fake better. How did
it work? In film review they would watch the linebackers and
safeties; the QB who duped the defense the most often would
win the game.

By the time the season rolled around Peyton had basically
mastered it. When he'd come out of the bootleg in practice the
back-side linebacker (the linebacker on the back side of the play
who was reading the quarterback) would roll out into the pass
coverage every time—even when Peyton had handed off the
ball. It didn't take long for Peyton to become probably the best
play-action quarterback of his era.

In Peyton's second season we decided to go no-huddle the
majority of the time. When the field is spread out with three
receivers, the game becomes simpler for most quarterbacks
because there are only so many things the QB can do. There
are also only so many things the defense can do, and Peyton
excelled at reading body language of defenders before the snap
and anticipating their actions.

Peyton flourished. He'd quickly read the defense and usually had the ball out of his hands in under three seconds. We put together code words and hand signals for him, and he learned them almost as fast as we could come up with them. His appetite for information was simply voracious.

This was how it worked: Tom Moore, our offensive coordinator, would call three plays and say "check-with-me." If the defense lined up in a certain way, Peyton would have the option to call a run to the right, a run to the left, or a pass because they overloaded the box. At the line the offensive players would "check with" Peyton to see which play he wanted.

It didn't take long for us to realize that Peyton was changing the game with his no-huddle brilliance. We gave him the keys to the car and he turned on the ignition and floored the gas pedal. Some quarterbacks can't handle this responsibility, but Peyton coveted it.

It takes a very intellectual quarterback to pull that off. Peyton always impressed me with his recall. One time during his rookie season we were playing the Washington Redskins and they showed us this unique "quarters coverage"—meaning they had four defensive backs lined up, each covering a quarter of the field.

A year later we were facing the Miami Dolphins when I noticed that exact same coverage alignment. I told Peyton, "You remember that Redskins game last year?"

He did—and he knew the exact play to beat it. On the sideline he grabbed his receivers and told them that if we got the four quarters coverage we were going to run "115 Divide Cross." This was a play-action bootleg. So Peyton would fake the handoff, bootleg to his right, one receiver would run to the pylon closest to Peyton, one would run a deep post route, and the other would take off on a deep cross. We knew the inside safety would run with that receiver on the crossing route to the pylon and the deep cross would be wide open.

Sure enough, on the next series, Peyton saw the four quarters coverage, called "115 Divide Cross," and hit Marvin Harrison for a touchdown. When Peyton reached the sideline he got on the phone with me in the press box. "Nice job, brother," I said, shaking my head.

"Yeah, we nailed that," he said, as if any quarterback could remember a random play of a year ago and use that knowledge to execute the perfect play call and score a TD to boot. Man, that was something.

That was the thing about coaching Peyton: You had to be totally prepared. Once you told him something, you never had to repeat yourself. That was why I still think he was my hardest quarterback to coach, because if you failed with him, it was on you as coach. You just couldn't overload his brain with information. It was like a massive maw.

Before coaching Peyton, I had always stayed in the office until my quarterbacks left the building, just in case they had a question. But Peyton would often stay in the quarterback meeting room deep into the night watching film. It got to the point that on Thursdays—which was my date night with my wife—I had to tell him, "I've got to take Chris to dinner, but she knows that if you call me and have a question I'll take the call and even leave if I have to." He never took me up on that offer, but it showed the level of commitment it took to coach him.

Peyton even obsessed over the game balls. On Saturdays after our walk-through practice, he'd wash his hands and then walk into the equipment room with our equipment manager. He'd shut the door so he could select his twelve game balls in silence, like it was some sort of ritual. He'd rub his hands over each ball. If he liked the feel of one, he'd toss it to the equipment manager and say, "Game," meaning the new ball was up to his lofty standards. If he didn't like the feel of it, he'd say, "Pregame," and rifle it to the other side of the room. That ball could only be used during warm-ups.

But it wasn't just Peyton's study habits and overall commitment that won over the team. He was an inveterate practical joker. He really loved messing with his backup quarterbacks. When Steve Walsh was his backup in 1999— Peyton's second year in the league—Steve brushed his teeth like ten times a day. So one day Peyton bought a toothbrush that looked just like Steve's. He then took a dump in the toilet, threw the toothbrush in there, and snapped a Polaroid of it. At lunch that afternoon he asked Steve if he had brushed his teeth that day. Steve said he had. Peyton slid the photo over to him, and Steve almost started throwing up. The entire lunchroom broke out in laughter.

Locker room jokes can be a little crude and disgusting, but they can build camaraderie and unity. Those guys in the locker room are your brothers, and you only pull practical jokes on people you care about. And Peyton was a master at winning the locker room over by being one of the guys and always looking for ways to playfully mess with other players.

Peyton became almost like a son to me. We were by each other's side for the first three years of his career. I could have stayed with him forever, we had such a strong bond. But I was a quarterback coach and I wanted to become an offensive coordinator. He knew what my goals were and he genuinely wanted me to succeed and continue climbing the NFL coaching ladder. Heck, I think he wanted that for me almost as much as I wanted it for myself.

When I got the offer to become the offensive coordinator of the Cleveland Browns following the 2001 season, it was very hard to say goodbye to Peyton. I called him on the phone and said, "It's been an unbelievable three years, but I need to go do this."

"I know, Coach," Peyton said. He then asked me who was going to be on the staff and what I thought about the quarterbacks on the Cleveland roster. That was typical of Peyton: He was as inquisitive as ever and concerned for his now former coach.

Finally, he said, "I can't wait to see what you can do."

Hanging up the phone, I felt like crying. I knew I'd probably never be so fortunate to coach another quarterback quite like Peyton Manning.

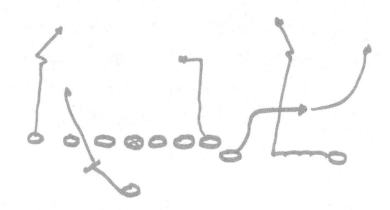

Bruce wants his quarterbacks to be able to throw
the ball down the field, of course, but you better
play smart or you won't be playing long for B.A.
Making good decisions is far more important
to him than anything else.
— ANDREW LUCK

CHAPTER 3

WHAT TO LOOK FOR IN A QB

The best quarterbacks to play in the NFL haven't been the biggest or the ones with the greatest arm strength. It's the guys with the greatest combination of grit, will, and brains—my most important ingredients when baking a successful NFL QB— who have flourished behind center.

When I was growing up in York, I watched the Baltimore Colts every Sunday afternoon. (York is only about fifty miles north of Baltimore.) They were my team, and Johnny Unitas was my quarterback, my human Superman. Today, when I visualize what a quarterback really is, the image I see is that of old Johnny U.

As a kid I knew his background about as well as my own. Coming out of the University of Louisville in 1955, he was drafted in the ninth round by his hometown Pittsburgh Steelers, but was released before the season even began. No other team gave him a chance, so he worked in construction to support his young family. On weekends he made six dollars a game playing in Pittsburgh sandlots for a semiprofessional team called the Bloomfield Rams.

In the summer of 1956 the Baltimore Colts offered him a tryout. He borrowed money from a friend to pay for the gas to make the drive from Pittsburgh. In training camp he impressed the Colts staff with his grit—as I said, that's my favorite quality of a quarterback—and his willingness to sacrifice his body for the team. He made the roster. After the Colts' starter, George Shaw, broke his leg in the second week of the season, Johnny trotted onto the field. Even though his first pass was intercepted and returned for a touchdown, the city of Baltimore would never be the same.

Unitas became the full-time starter in '57 and led the league passing yards (2,550) and touchdown passes (24). That season he won the first of his four league MVP awards. In '58 he played the second half of the season with three broken ribs—every throw had to hurt—but he still battled on and led the Colts to only their second winning season since their founding in 1953. What's more, he guided them to victory over the New York Giants on December 28 in the first-ever NFL Championship Game to go to sudden-death overtime.

On that raw afternoon at Yankee Stadium, Johnny U threw a touchdown strike to Raymond Berry to lead Baltimore to a 23–17 win in what became known as "the Greatest Game Ever Played." An estimated 45 million people watched the game on TV that day. Two years later the American Football League was formed. A decade later it merged with the NFL, creating the juggernaut that pro football has become.

And remember this important thing: Unitas didn't have an offensive coordinator or a quarterback coach in the press box telling him what plays he should call or what defensive alignment he should expect. Instead, Johnny U called his own plays in the huddle, came to the line in his tall black cleats, diagnosed the defense, checked to another play when necessary, and then handed the ball off or dropped back to pass. And when he did take a five- or seven-step drop, he seemed totally unaware of the chaos that frequently was about to envelop him. He kept his eyes downfield at all times, standing tall and looking poised and resolute. Johnny U was as courageous as any quarterback I've ever seen.

Was Unitas the greatest athlete? No. Did he have the strongest arm? No. Was he an elite competitor? Yes. And was he one of the all-time smartest quarterbacks in NFL history? No question.

One day when I was an eighth grader at St. Mary's a few of the Colts players—including Johnny Unitas—played members of our faculty in a basketball game. I couldn't take my eyes off Johnny. Other times I'd watch a few Colt players drink beer at Mon's Café in York, where a bunch of them hung out. These were the first times I was close to professional football players, and I could see the tight bond they had. It inspired me; I wanted to be a player just like them, to be a part of a professional team. Every Sunday I'd jiggle the rabbit ears antenna that sat atop our black-and-white television so I could watch my heroes play their games. Johnny was my idol.

When I played quarterback at Virginia Tech, Dan Henning was our offensive coordinator. He taught us to throw by mimicking Unitas's overhand motion. It seems so simple—you receive the snap, you grip the ball, you drop back to pass, you set up in the pocket, you rifle the ball down the field. But the art of throwing is so much more complex than that.

With Unitas, every throw was always in rhythm and every throw had a purpose. He didn't generate the most velocity, but he always released the ball at the top of his motion—if his motion was overlaid on a clock face, he'd consistently release the ball at high noon—and his follow-through was straight down, textbook-perfect. Johnny wasn't a thrower; he was a passer. You always want passers, not throwers. Throwers wait to see a receiver break open and then sling it in that direction, usually as hard as they can. Passers release the ball before the receivers get open, usually with the right velocity and touch.

How do you teach someone to become a passer? It's all about anticipation, knowing the limitations of your arm, and developing the optimum throwing motion. Unitas was the master at that. My favorite play to watch was a little out-cut pattern he'd toss to wide receiver Raymond Berry, a play where Berry would run a few yards down the field then turn sharply toward the sideline. Even as Berry would still be running his route, his back to his quarterback, Unitas would unleash the ball. Just as Berry was nearing the sideline the ball would arrive in his hands as if by magic. He'd tap his feet inbounds and the Colts would gain eleven yards. That play was wizardry in motion.

And it had nothing to do with the zip that Unitas put on the ball; it was simple timing, which Unitas and Berry practiced for hours. If either the quarterback or the receiver is only slightly off in their movements, those types of plays will result in incompletions or interceptions. The receiver can't get to his spot too soon or too late and the quarterback can't deliver the ball to him too soon or too late. It's an incredibly fragile formula. It demands repetition and precision and sweat.

There have been so many other great quarterbacks in the NFL who didn't have big-league arms. Otto Graham led the Cleveland Browns to the league championship game every year between 1946 and '55—the Browns won seven of those games—but he was only 6'1" and didn't weigh 200 pounds. He was a winner, finishing his career with an astounding 105–17–4 regular-season record. He was smart too: He was one of the first quarterbacks in NFL history with enough sense to play with a face mask on his helmet.

I met "Automatic Otto" in 2001 after a Saturday morning walkthrough practice in Cleveland. Even then, at age seventy-nine, the guy still oozed confidence. "You know, I never threw a bad pass in my life," he told me. "Even the ones that got intercepted, in my mind, should have hit the receiver in the chest if he'd run the right pattern." Now that's the attitude of a winner!

Graham had the "it" factor that most successful quarterbacks possess. The most famously confident quarterback was Joe Namath, who guaranteed the Jets would win Super Bowl III against the Colts even though New York was an 18-point underdog according to the oddsmakers in Las Vegas. He showed them, completing 17 of 28 passes for 206 yards and guiding the Jets to a 16–7 victory.

I met Joe when I was coaching at the University of Alabama in 1981. His college coach, Bear Bryant, was being inducted into the Alabama Sports Hall of Fame, and Joe and I talked for a few minutes before the ceremony. He was the embodiment of cool. When my wife, Chris, walked over and joined our conversation, he took a long look at her, then shifted his eyes back to me. Smiling mischievously, he said, "Boy, you outkicked your coverage."

After Joe walked away, I asked Chris, "Would you leave me for him?"

It took all of two heartbeats for her to respond. "Yes!" she yelled just a little too enthusiastically. But I swear, Joe invented the word "swagger" years before it became part of our everyday language. He was the ultimate Swag and that's how he played. No risk it, no biscuit. I got my motto from Joe.

You need to have the right persona to flourish as a quarterback in the NFL. Johnny Unitas was clean-cut and the most determined SOB on the field. Joe was "Broadway Joe" who never truly believed he was going to lose. Peyton was "the Piranha" whose never-ending pursuit of information he would use to bite his opponents.

Another quarterback who had great skills and unique demeanor was Kenny Stabler, who went 96–49–1 as a starting NFL quarterback with the Raiders, Oilers, and Saints—a .661 winning percentage. He made plays that become so famous they took on their own names: the Holy Roller, the Sea of Hands, the Ghost to the Post. He was a swashbuckling outlaw of a quarterback; he didn't mind having a drink or twelve with the boys after a big win. In his prime during the late 1970s with the Raiders, he was a larger-than-life figure, even though he didn't have the strongest of arms.

It was his attitude that was infectious. I met him in the early 1990s when I was back coaching at Alabama and was on a recruiting trip to Mobile. We bumped into each other at the Flora-Bama bar. Man, he was one cool dude. After talking to him for just a few minutes, as a band played onstage in the background, I remember thinking I would follow this guy anywhere. He lived hard and played harder—and his teammates loved him. There was no BS to the guy.

Bottom line: About 95 percent of the successful quarterbacks in the NFL are special *people*, not just robots with big arms. They inspire others. They get teammates to do things they never thought possible. You want to be around that kind of quarterback. It's hard to find people who have the grit—the physical and mental skills and the strength of character—of successful NFL quarterbacks. Sure as hell there are not many in business or academia or politics. But once you cross paths with someone like this, it sticks with you for the rest of your life.

When you're in the presence of someone who possesses these qualities, it's almost like seeing a rare comet streaking through the night sky. You want to hold on to the moment for as long as you can, because you know once it's gone, it may be years before you spot the likes of that person again.

Parents approach me all the time asking the same question: *What can I do right now to prepare my son to be an NFL quarterback?* Here's what I tell them.

It begins with developing a work ethic. Teach him that nothing in life is handed to anyone, that anything worth achieving takes consistent effort and relentless dedication. If a boy dreams of playing quarterback in the league, then he needs to be the first to arrive at every Pop Warner practice and be the first in line for every drill. He needs to be the last to leave the field once the practice is over and he should beg his coach and teammates to stick around afterward to work on fundamentals. This is not a secret: Sustained effort toward developing and maintaining mental and physical skills is the foundation upon which success in life is built.

I also tell parents that their son shouldn't play only one sport, because kids need to develop all their muscles, and the best way to achieve that is by having their kid play football, basketball, soccer, baseball—as many sports as he has time for. I know that a lot of high-level college coaches won't even look at high school quarterbacks who only play football, because there is a widespread belief in coaching circles that if a kid only focuses on football, he'll have maxed out his potential by the time he reaches college. But if kids play multiple sports, the logic goes, their ability to grow as athletes will be far greater when they step onto a college campus. So in my view, the more sports boys play in junior high and high school the better chance they'll have to make it to the NFL one day. And even then, they'll have to overcome long, long odds. Remember, of the roughly 1 million kids who play high school football each year, only about 200 will ever make it onto an NFL roster. Even if you only make it as far as high school quarterback, you've learned to lead men. You're a success.

It's also important, I tell them, to cultivate within a child at a very young age the belief that he or she is not going to fail.

This has nothing to do with sports, really, but everything to do with your kid's mental approach. How do you create that attitude in your child? By teaching the value of work and the need to be prepared. Because when your kid is as prepared as possible, he should believe—not just think—he'll succeed. He'll have already done more work than anyone else in that game.

Everyone doesn't win, but that's not failing. And you don't necessarily succeed right away. You might be benched, you might get kicked out of school like yours truly, and you might get hurt. The key is to always get back up and keep fighting.

And trust me, if a boy aspires to become an NFL quarterback, the path of development usually begins around age twelve. That's when the special kids learn how to pay "the price" it will take; how to outwork everyone else their age and understand the value of doing that as well.

Then, as your son progresses from Pop Warner football through middle school football to early high school football, I think it's a good idea to find a football mentor, a working coach or former successful college or pro player who can teach your son how to pass the ball, not throw it. The good quarterback tutor will tirelessly show and work him through the fundamentals of ball handling and passing. He'll teach him footwork, balance, and throwing mechanics. He'll explain how to manage the offense and how to read and manipulate the defense.

But parents need to be realists. If their son is 5'8", 145 pounds as a high school senior, he's probably not going to be the next Tom Brady or Peyton Manning or Aaron Rodgers— no matter how much his mom and dad believe he will be. It's not the job of a parent to shatter the dreams of their children, certainly, but neither they nor their kids should live in a false reality. I say let kids discover their physical limitations on their own, but never, ever stop encouraging them to aspire to succeed. Succeeding isn't being Peyton Manning; it's being the best you can be.

That is what I did with my son, Jake. I was coaching at Temple University at the time. One afternoon when he was eight, we were sitting in our living room in New Jersey and he said, "Dad, I'm going to play in the NFL."

Of course, I thought he was living in a fantasy world, but I told him that anything is possible if you work hard enough. Then I asked him if he even knew what the NFL was. "Yes, Pops!" he proclaimed. "It's the Eagles, the Bears, the Packers, the Giants, the Steelers . . ." He named nearly every team in the league along with dozens of players.

"Okay," I told him. "But if you don't start picking your grades up, you're not going to play college football and you definitely won't make it to the NFL." Almost overnight, Jake's grades started improving. He had his goal; his mind was set.

After I got fired as head coach at Temple in December 1988, I was hired to coach the running backs with the Kansas City Chiefs. We placed Jake in a junior high school in Missouri that happened to be predominantly white. At fourteen he stood 5'7" and weighed 140 pounds. He played quarterback and safety. He was a good player, but it wasn't like he was on a path to becoming a blue-chip recruit.

In 1993, I became the offensive coordinator at Mississippi State. Jake moved to a new, mostly black high school in Starkville, Mississippi, and played on a high school team that featured two future first-round draft picks. One evening Jake, then a sophomore, came home from practice and told me, "Dad, I think I need to learn how to kick. These dudes are *soooooo* fast." From that moment, he spent hours each day working on kicking and punting.

He was something of a natural at both. He had taken karate lessons starting at age five. My rule was, when you sign up, you go full-term. Even if you don't like it, you finish what you started and you don't stop until the lessons are over. Jake agreed, and I went to as many of his practices and tournaments as I could.

One evening a year later, I walked into our house and asked six-year-old Jake to show me what he had learned that day at karate. And in an eye blink, that little squirt kicked my feet out from under me and I landed hard on my back. I muttered in a whisper, "Good shit, son." He killed me. By age eight, he could do leg splits.

I think karate really helped him with his kicking, because he had developed so much flexibility. Jake later earned a kicking scholarship to the University of Alabama–Birmingham, and in 2001 he made the roster of the Buffalo Bills. He achieved his dream; he became an NFL player—at 5'10" and 200 pounds. Jake didn't last the season with the Bills, his only NFL team, but he had reached his personal summit. It was the journey that was important, not the fact that he didn't stay in the league for long. He willed himself into becoming an NFL player, and it was a testament to his determination that he made it. That was the life lesson takeaway—and what made me as his father so damn proud.

How did he do it? It sure as hell wasn't genetics. He did it because he played multiple sports as a kid—along with karate, he excelled at soccer as a boy, which ended up helping him when he later focused on becoming a kicker—and because he had an internal motor that never stopped red-lining.

Those are some of the primary attributes that Jake acquired and all the great NFL QBs have in common. One other vital trait they all shared? They simply outworked everyone else.

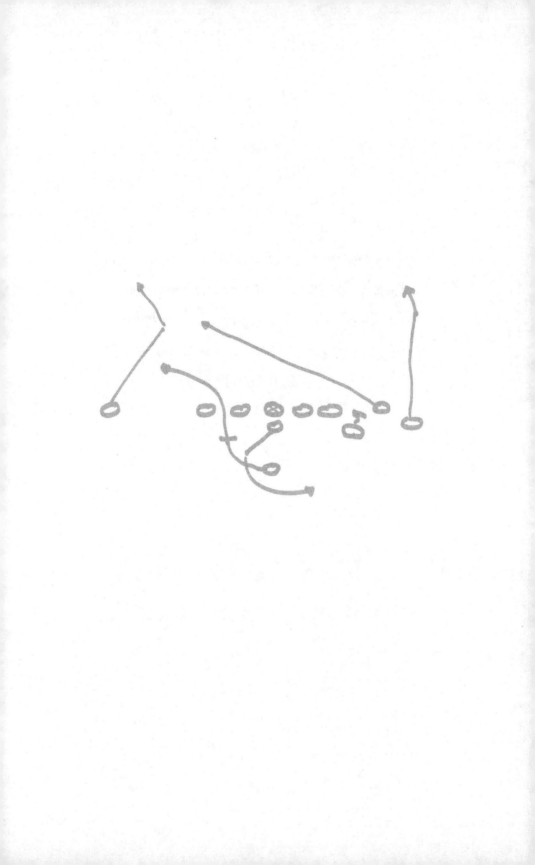

What sets Bruce apart is that he can get you to do things you didn't think you were necessarily capable of. And it's all because he really cares about you and, in return, you want to make him proud.

— KELLY HOLCOMB

CHAPTER 4

KELLY HOLCOMB

There is nothing more gratifying in coaching than helping a player reach his potential. Oh yeah, getting there can be a helluva process: sometimes short and sweet, sometimes long and agonizing. But when potential is finally and fully realized, the experience is really special, like how an artist must feel when all the various individual brushstrokes on the canvas merge to form a beautiful painting.

That is why one of the favorite days of my career was January 5, 2003—a snowy afternoon in Pittsburgh that remains as vivid to me as any game in my career. This was a day all the brushstrokes of effort came together for Kelly Holcomb.

I was the offensive coordinator for the Cleveland Browns. In the second quarter of our final regular-season game against the Atlanta Falcons, our starting quarterback, Tim Couch, broke his leg. It was a devastating injury for the team and for Tim. A former number one overall draft choice, Tim had been playing well. He had put us on the verge of making the playoffs for the first time in nine years. Yet all season the Cleveland fans were rough on him—it seemed like they booed him even when he threw completions. But I'll tell you, Tim Couch was not a bust. His body became busted, but he was no bust. There's a big difference.

After Tim went down in that last game, our backup, Kelly Holcomb, replaced him. Kelly hadn't played in over two months, but he threw a late touchdown pass to Kevin Johnson to give us the lead, and we won the game 24–16. We made the playoffs as a wild card. Our opponent in the first round: the Pittsburgh Steelers.

Kelly had been with me in Indianapolis from 1998 to 2000. When I first saw him play against the Vikings the year before I joined the Colts staff, he was atrocious. He didn't know where to go with the ball, had trouble reading defenses, and generally looked totally bewildered, like he couldn't find his ass with two hands and a search warrant. I feared he was a lost cause.

But I loved Kelly's competitive fire—and the fact he had a chip the size of a boulder on his shoulder, just like me. There were plenty of times in my career when I thought I had it all together and I got a bit cocky, a little nonchalant. Kelly was like that too.

He came into our first quarterbacks meeting in Indianapolis along with Peyton Manning. I looked at Kelly and was shocked—he didn't even have a notebook, for godsakes! Peyton had five. "Where's your notebook?" I asked. He didn't have a good answer. But he learned how to prepare simply by watching Peyton and emulating his actions.

It wasn't long before Kelly started staying at the facility with Peyton to review plays and defenses into the evening hours. Peyton made other quarterbacks want to be as prepared as he was. Hey, sometimes peer pressure can be positive. Kelly picked up on that.

Every Friday before practice we all played what we called "the Goal Post Game." One of us would stand at the five-yard line and try to hit the goalpost; the other two would stand underneath the goalpost and try to catch it after it bounced off. Then they would move back to the 10-yard line, the 15, the 20, and finally the 25.

Peyton was so accurate that he'd hit the goalpost dead on almost every time, so the ball would drop straight down, making it easy to catch. If you caught the ball, it meant the throwing quarterback lost five points.

Kelly was almost as accurate, but his balls usually veered off to the left or right after hitting the post. Peyton rarely beat Kelly in this game, because he was so damn precise with his throws. But Kelly's accuracy improved dramatically in short order. He could hit the goalpost almost every time from every distance.

In games, however, he struggled with deep balls. He just didn't have the proper touch. But again, Peyton's work ethic rubbed off on him. He worked like a maniac on his fundamentals. We really stressed shuffling around in the pocket to avoid the rush, resetting his feet, then throwing the ball down the field with accuracy. To replicate a game situation at practices, I'd have three defenders run at him. Then we had three managers ten to twenty yards downfield, spread out at the numbers to the sideline. While Kelly avoided the rush, I would yell, "Ball!" as I pointed at one of the managers, indicating for him to put his hands up. At that moment Kelly had to reset his feet and immediately throw to the manager who had his arms extended. This replicated a game environment. Every day, every practice, he improved.

I always like to have a backup quarterback who knows my system. The solid backup is another coach in the meeting room and on the field. Remember, quarterbacks will ask their fellow quarterbacks more questions than they'll ever ask their own coaches. It's just like in school—students are more likely to ask other students questions before raising their hand to ask the teacher. So when I was hired by the Browns in 2001, I insisted to our general manager that we sign Kelly, who was then a free agent. When I got the green light to get Kelly, I immediately called him. He was in his car driving to Cincinnati and he told me he was on his way to signing a contract with the Bengals. "Damn it, you better turn left off the highway instead of right and come to Cleveland," I said. "Remember, you're in this league because of me."

I hated to pull that card on him, but he ended up turning left and drove to Cleveland. We signed him the next day.

It was important to me to have Kelly on our roster, because he and I had built the one thing that is more important between a coach and player than anything else: trust. It's so hard to establish that in the NFL. It's done through the work you do together, the hours you spend side by side doing the drills and watching film. It's a lot like a golfer and his swing coach. There are so many minute aspects of a golf swing that need to be perfect for a golfer to play at his best. It's the same thing with a coach and his quarterback. Both must work long and hard on mechanics so they become automatic mentally and second nature physically for the QB, because he has so many other things to worry about when on the field. Mastered mechanics—footwork, dropbacks, looking off defenders, ball grip, arm swing, and touch, for example—free a quarterback to think about how the defense is lining up, what his hot read is going to be, and what protection he needs to call. The QB must be concerned about these bigger things, not whether or not the ball is going to come out of his hand cleanly.

Every new season in Indy we brought in backup quarterbacks to try to beat out Kelly—Stoney Case, Billy Joe Hobert, and Steve Walsh. It wasn't personal to Kelly; we merely wanted to challenge him. Plus, the NFL is a harsh Darwinian world. No matter how much you might like a quarterback, if you can find a better one, you sign him, because that's for the betterment of the team. Besides, the "better ones" are pretty damn rare.

Kelly handled every competition with class. He always helped the other quarterbacks in our meeting room and on the practice field. He was a true pro, which made me like him even more.

Plus, I could see a little bit of myself in Kelly. He was a fighter, a scrapper, the kind of guy you want by your side in a dark alley.

Kelly was a country kid. He grew up in Fayetteville, Tennessee, a town of about 7,000. His dad, John, played baseball in high school, and his mom, Amy, was a star basketball player in high school. Kelly inherited athletic genes.

As his dad worked construction, Kelly would constantly be in the yard throwing a football to his mom and playing pickup games with other kids. When he was twelve the family moved to a farm three miles outside of town. Kelly took up hunting; he bagged his first ten-point buck before he was even a teenager.

In sixth grade Kelly announced to his father that he wanted to go out for football. His dad was skeptical. Kelly was rail thin, and his father didn't know if he could survive a season. Plus, his dad feared that after his son took a few big licks, he'd lose his desire to play the game. So he told Kelly what I told my son, Jake: "If you start the season, you play the entire season, no matter what. You're not going to quit."

Kelly agreed. "Dad," he said, "I'll never quit. I promise."

And so began his football career. He was a tireless worker. After school he'd come and convince his mom to play catch with him. For hours on end, the two of them would toss the ball back and forth. Amy eventually had to bow out of these backyard games; her son was gunning the ball so hard it was breaking her fingernails.

By the time Kelly was in high school he was on the baseball team and could throw a 90-plus-MPH fastball. He was an all-conference pitcher and shortstop. But then he fell in love with football, and that became his top priority. He tied an old rubber tire to a rafter in their barn and threw footballs at that tire for hours on end, minutely adjusting his grip, changing his arm motion, differing the velocity of the ball. He couldn't get enough of learning how to spin a tight spiral through a small space.

In his junior year the starting quarterback went down with an injury. Kelly trotted onto the field. The team had been running the option, but the head coach started calling passing plays for Kelly, who then weighed all of 155 pounds. He proceeded to light up defenses the rest of the season. As a high school senior, he led his team to a 15–0 record and a state championship.

But it was off the field where Kelly really shined. One time, the team's starting tight end wanted to skip practice to spend time with his girlfriend. This didn't sit well with Kelly. He confronted the bigger player. Kelly ended up with a cut on his chin, but the tight end scrapped his plans with his girl and instead went to practice. This is what leadership looks like.

I knew all of this about Kelly the day I met him, which made me inclined to like him. He had flourished in multiple sports in high school—a key ingredient for future NFL success—and was country tough and back-alley smart.

He desperately wanted to play for Alabama, but the Tide coaches looked at his skinny six-foot frame—as a high school senior he couldn't have weighed more than 170 pounds—and didn't offer him a full ride. So he signed with Middle Tennessee State. In his first scrimmage he was knocked silly by a truck of a linebacker, but only minutes later he begged his head coach to go back onto the field. In his sophomore year a defender crushed him in an early game and he played most of his season with his jaw wired shut. Heck, he could barely talk and had to drink milkshakes for his meals—but he kept playing. The kid was a fighter. He had grit.

Kelly went undrafted in 1995, but signed as a free agent with Tampa Bay. He was cut. He eventually landed a job at Anheuser-Busch, where he helped build a boat dock for a brewery. But he wasn't ready for a nine-to-five lifestyle. So in 1996 he played in the World League for the Barcelona Dragons. He played well enough to earn a shot with the Colts, and he made the team. He was a player I could work with.

We had signed him with the Browns in March 2001. I knew, given the right circumstances, that Kelly could succeed in the NFL. At first he was our backup. I wanted him in the quarterbacks' room because he knew my system. He spent hours working with our starter, Tim Couch, poring over the playbook and teaching Tim the intricacies of my offense. He embraced his role and helped Tim play the best football of his NFL career.

But then when Tim went down late in the 2002–03 season, Kelly was ready for prime time. On January 5, 2003, on that snowy afternoon in Pittsburgh in the first round of the playoffs, this journeyman quarterback was transformed into a veritable Hall of Famer—all because he had spent years preparing for the moment. For sixty minutes of action, hell, he looked like the second coming of Otto Graham.

I had been in this kind of situation before.

In the spring of 1978, I was the passing game coordinator at Mississippi State. I spent spring practice searching for a starting quarterback. But all the signal callers I had on the roster really struggled. I feared we wouldn't win a single game in the SEC. And if that happened, I knew what it meant—my fledgling coaching career might be over. I was twenty-five and had a young family to provide for—Jake was in diapers. Shit, we were living in a dorm room. I was desperate.

Then, one afternoon in the sticky spring heat, I saw our kicker, Dave Marler, pick up a ball on the practice field. He threw a pass to another player. That sounds like a simple act, but I was immediately transfixed. The ball flew out of his arm in a gorgeous spiral, and he looked far more natural throwing that pass than any of the quarterbacks I had been teaching.

Marler was listed as our fifth-string quarterback and I admit I hadn't been paying much attention to him. Then one Saturday we held a scrimmage. We couldn't make a first down on offense. I was extremely frustrated and was silently wondering just how long this season was going to be. Then I remembered seeing Marler throw that pass. I asked the other coaches to put him into the scrimmage and line him up behind center.

They thought I was nuts until Dave uncorked his first ball—a tight spiral that hit the receiver in stride. Even though he was our starting kicker, Dave led us down the field on his first possession and we scored. Then he did it again. Suddenly I'm thinking to myself, *We've got something to work with here.*

But it wasn't just that he had a beautiful throwing stroke; it was clear that he could read the defense, he could process the needed information, and by God he knew what to do with that information. Over and over during the scrimmage, he threw the ball to the correct receiver based on the coverage the defense played.

Plus, Dave was hungry and had an edge to him—two characteristics I love in quarterbacks. He grew up in central Mississippi and as a boy dreamed of one thing—playing quarterback for the Mississippi State Bulldogs in Starkville.

But head coach Bob Tyler didn't offer Dave a scholarship. Tyler didn't believe he had the physical attributes to be a successful SEC quarterback. So Dave headed to Mississippi College in Clinton, a small Division II school at the time. He played quarterback and was the team's first-string kicker. But he never relinquished his dream. After two years, he transferred to Mississippi State to be the Bulldogs' kicker.

I didn't really even know who he was until that day in spring practice when I saw him throw that innocuous pass on the practice field. But then I dug into his background and quickly realized he had one of the skills I demand out of my quarterbacks: desire—abundant desire. When a quarterback has that, you know you have something to work with. So I had my lump of clay. Now I just needed to sculpt it on the potter's wheel.

Even though I was relatively new to coaching—shoot, I was only four years older than Dave—I had done that once before. In my first year as a graduate assistant at Virginia Tech my primary task was to transform Phil Rogers, who had been our leading rusher when I was a senior, into a wishbone quarterback.

I spent hours with Phil studying the playbook and analyzing opposing defenses. I tutored him on simple things like how to get his teammates lined up, how to voice his cadence at the line of scrimmage, and how to properly receive the snap. I worked endlessly on refining his throwing motion and his footwork. Running our wishbone attack, Phil wasn't always the prettiest quarterback to watch, but he did lead us to an 8–3 record. He wound up rushing for 762 yards and passing for 379. It wasn't easy, but we made a quarterback of him.

Now I tried to do the same thing with Dave Marler— the second quarterback project of my career—at Mississippi State. We started, as always, with the fundamentals. In one drill I stood ten yards behind the goalpost and Dave stood ten yards in front of it. I wanted him to throw the ball over the ten-foot-high crossbar so that it would hit me squarely in the chest. He needed to thread the ball as close to the post as possible without hitting it.

At first, Dave struggled. He'd overthrow me or the ball would sail underneath the post. But we kept at it for about two weeks, a hundred throws a day. Pass by pass, he improved. My goal for him was to perfect his throwing motion and increase both his arm strength and his accuracy. The ten-foot-high crossbar is an important marker; it replicates how high a quarterback will need to throw the ball, with velocity, to get it over leaping defensive linemen and linebackers who drop back into coverage, but in front of the safeties.

At the same time that we performed these drills, I taught Dave how to read SEC defenses. So much of this aspect of the game falls on the quarterback and his desire to learn. This is why a coach always wants a quarterback who has something to prove—who believes he has somehow been wronged—because he is typically going to want to do everything in his power to succeed. And Dave was an ideal student; first, he absorbed everything I said; and then at night, alone in his dorm room, he'd stay up at his desk with his head bowed under a circle of lamplight and he'd review everything we had discussed as if he was cramming for the most important final exam of his life. This is another example of grit.

We opened the season against West Texas A&M in Jackson, Mississippi. The coaching staff kept everything simple for Dave; the last thing we wanted was for him to overthink on the field and suffer paralysis by analysis, a common malady for young quarterbacks. We pared down the playbook and Dave was terrific, leading us to a 28–0 win.

The next week we traveled to North Texas State. We again employed a rudimentary game plan and Dave thrived in our bare-bones offensive system. We won 17–5. Fourteen days later, with Dave becoming more confident and more comfortable behind center, we expanded our repertoire of offensive plays against Memphis State. We cruised to a 44–14 victory. Dave—our kicker, our former fifth-string quarterback—now led the SEC in several passing categories.

To nurture Dave's growing confidence, I began telling him every day, "Dave, you're the best quarterback in the SEC. You're the best damn quarterback in the league!" Everyone in life needs reassurance, but quarterbacks especially so. You want to eliminate all doubt in the quarterback's mind. In late October we beat Tennessee 34–21 at the Liberty Bowl in Memphis. The following week we bused to Birmingham, Alabama, to face the third-ranked Crimson Tide and their legendary coach Bear Bryant at Legion Field. This, we knew, was going to be our biggest challenge of the season.

We anticipated the Alabama defense playing what's called a "zero coverage blitz." We figured they would blitz us virtually every play, sending one more guy than we could block. But this also meant that they were covering each of our wide receivers man-to-man with only one defensive back. So if our quarterback had time to throw, our receiver should in theory be able to beat his guy and get open.

How could we exploit this? We practiced the single-wing shotgun—the quarterback lined up seven yards behind center, usually with a fullback and tailback set off to his left and a wingback to his right—with four basic quick-pass patterns; the idea was to throw it before the extra defender reached Dave. We felt great about this old-school attack that was the precursor to the modern spread formation and that that no one in the country was running. We were, it turns out, ahead of our time.

During pregame warm-ups when Dave was kicking he felt a pop in his right thigh. He limped over to me and with a determined look and forceful words in his voice, said, "Coach, I can stand still and throw it." I found out minutes later from our trainer that Dave had partially torn a muscle, but the trainer said he could play . . . if Dave could withstand the pain.

Dave promised me he could. I then told him to act like nothing was wrong; I didn't want to tip off Alabama that our quarterback could barely run. Minutes before kickoff he hobbled into the locker room, where the trainers quickly wrapped his leg. He returned and entered the game shortly after the start of the first quarter, but he was sacked on his first possession and aggravated the injury. Now he could barely walk. I'm up in the press box and it's obvious to me—and to everyone in the stadium—that our starting quarterback has about as much mobility as my one-year-old.

One of the cardinal rules of coaching is never panic. Never.

Don't get me wrong: We were prepared for the zero blitz—as long as Dave could stand back there and throw. But now we had to run our entire offense, not just the pass plays, out of the shotgun. Of course, we didn't have time to go over this. So now we just used the four quick passes we worked on in practice.

Meantime, up in the press box, I'm feverishly drawing the rest of the plays on loose pieces of paper. I must have sketched out fifteen running and passing plays that we now needed to run out of the shotgun. In the locker room at halftime I gathered the offense and went over the different plays I had just jotted down. I'm talking a blue streak, telling everyone our plan for the final thirty minutes of the game. I was coaching by the seat of my pants, but looking back, that probably was the most fun I ever had in a game.

We came out in the second half and Dave was brilliant, picking apart the Crimson Tide with surgical precision. Against one of the best defenses in the nation, our immobile kicker-turned-passer threw for a school record 429 yards, the most Alabama gave up through the air all season. We lost 35–14, but I must have made some type of impression on Bear Bryant. He hired me a little more than two years later.

Dave ended up leading the SEC that season in ten different offensive categories, and we set forty-seven school records and fifteen conference records on offense. And our starting kicker was named All-SEC quarterback. Dave broke Steve Spurrier's record for consecutive completions with seventeen straight, and he even passed Archie Manning on the SEC's all-time single-season total offense list. Dave took his confidence and the skills he learned at Mississippi State and ended up playing five years in the CFL.

Did I sprinkle pixie dust on Dave? Absolutely not. He had all that potential inside him, and he was willing—indeed, downright determined—to bust his tail to bring it out. I was just his coach who helped him fulfill a different and fuller potential.

The playoff game on January 5, 2003, against the Steelers had a midafternoon kickoff. As the offensive coordinator for the Browns, I always met with my quarterbacks the night before the game. The evening before we faced the Steelers, we went over the game plan—as we always did—and I let Kelly Holcomb select his favorite plays, which I then worked into our script of thirty opening plays.

Some TV analysts will say that it's always good to start the game with an easy throw—such as a wide receiver screen—to give quarterback confidence. I don't buy that. I want my quarterback to execute his favorite plays early in the game, no matter how difficult the throws may be. If it's a bomb, then we're calling a bomb on the first play. If it's a play-action pass, then we're calling that. The idea is to make your quarterback comfortable, and the best way to do that is to run his favorite plays. You want to get your QB into an early rhythm. Throwing a little screen pass on the first play doesn't do that.

We had already played Pittsburgh twice, and they had beaten us by three points each matchup. So Kelly knew precisely what he was going up against. He understood that the Steeler cornerbacks consistently bit on double moves by our wide receivers. So we believed we would have plenty of chances to beat them on deep throws. This was one reason why I was so excited about this game; we were going to sling the ball all over the field and play the kind of wide-open football that I love the most—the kind of game that Dave Marler and I had played against Alabama a quarter century earlier.

Kelly and I also were in tune with the body language of the Steelers defense. For instance, we knew that when linebacker Jason Gildon lined up with his feet facing directly at the quarterback he was going to blitz. And when his feet were pointed in a different direction it meant he would drop into coverage and the blitz would come from the other side of the field. So at the line of scrimmage, Kelly would read Gildon's feet and either switch the protection to the opposite side or keep the play as we had called it.

We won the coin toss and elected to receive—we wanted to show the Steelers that we were confident we could move the ball against their defense, even though we were underdogs. To put it more plainly, we wanted to go after them. In the opening minute, I called a deep pass to wide receiver Kevin Johnson. As we had predicted in our meeting, the Pittsburgh corner bit on Johnson's double move and Kelly

delivered a beautiful ball into his arms. The pass went for 83
yards and set up a short touchdown run by William Green.
With snow falling from the cold midwestern sky, we were up
7–0 only minutes after the last notes of the national anthem
had been belted out.

That opening shock and awe immediately put pressure on
Pittsburgh, which is another reason why I think quick-strike
long balls early in games are so crucial. It sets a tone that can
be hard for the other team to shake—their players know it,
their coaches know it, even their knowledgeable fans know it.
We seized on this early momentum against the Steelers. Kelly
had 232 passing yards by halftime and early in the third quarter we held a 17-point lead.

The game slowed down for Kelly. A gifted basketball
player like Michael Jordan calls that being "in the zone,"
and man, was Kelly in it. He started out on fire and played
that way the entire game. He flung balls deep with accuracy
at Heinz Field. He feathered intermediate-length passes with
touch between defenders and into the arms of his target. And
he sprayed fastballs all around the field that hit his receivers
between the numbers.

Kelly simply saw everything that the Steelers were doing
and knew precisely how to solve every challenge they threw
at him. For example, he understood, based on how they
lined up, when they were going to blitz and who his hot read
was going to be. Kelly was so into the game plan that he
instinctively knew what play I was going to call before I radioed it into his headset. This may have been the easiest game
I ever called.

With three minutes left in the fourth quarter, we had the ball and were leading 33–29. It was third-and-12. The Steelers were out of timeouts. I thought a corner route to Dennis Northcutt would be open, and it was. If Dennis catches the ball, it's a first down, kneeldown, game over. But Dennis tried to run with the ball before he had secured it, and the pass bounced off his hands and onto the snow-wet grass. The Steelers scored a touchdown with less than a minute to play and we lost 36–33.

Dennis felt terrible about dropping that pass. I hate to play the "what if" game, but if we had beaten the Steelers we would have played the Raiders in the next round of the play-offs. The Raiders had three defensive backs out with injuries, and we were a three-wide-receiver offense. There is zero doubt in my mind that we would have lit them up like the night sky on the Fourth of July. We would have moved on to the AFC Championship Game and then, well, who knows? Maybe I would have even gotten an interview to become a head coach.

But that game against Pittsburgh will always be special to me. Kelly threw for 429 yards, the most ever in a wild-card game and third most in NFL postseason history at the time.

But Kelly's magic for us didn't end there. The next season, on September 21, 2003, we traveled to San Francisco to play the 49ers in an early-season game. Kelly had beaten out Tim Couch for the starting job, but our offense really struggled; we lost our first two games, and we fell behind the 49ers 12–0. Early in the fourth quarter we had the ball in San Francisco territory when I called a quarterback sneak on a third-down play. Kelly got hit hard in the leg and he was limping so badly he could barely walk. Still, he threw a two-yard touchdown pass to André Davis to narrow the score to 12–7.

Kelly approached me on the sideline. "My leg is fucked up," he said.

"What do you want to do?" I asked. "Can you still play?"

"I'm not coming out," he said.

Well, we got the ball back at our nine-yard line with time running out. Kelly could hardly move in the pocket, but he started throwing darts all over the field. Once again, it reminded me of Marler against Alabama; Kelly just carved up the 49er defense. His teammates could obviously see he was hurt—hell, the entire stadium could see that—but Kelly ignored his own pain because he knew his team needed him. He moved us down the field and with less than a minute to play he hit André Davis for an 11-yard touchdown pass. We won 13–12. On that final drive, as he was wincing and grunting in pain, Kelly had completed 12 of 14 passes.

This was one of the grittiest performances I'd ever seen from one of my quarterbacks. He willed us to the win. Kelly's entire life, dating back to when he was a skinny kid growing up in Tennessee and getting the piss beat out of him in Pee Wee football, had prepared him to succeed at this critical moment.

We didn't know it until we returned to Cleveland, but Kelly had played that entire final drive with a broken leg. An X-ray revealed that he had a hairline fracture in his right leg. Man, talk about toughness.

"Everybody needs a guy that believes in him, and Bruce made me believe I could do anything," Kelly says. "When

it came to Xs and Os, Bruce made his money by designing play-action passes that could really hurt defenses. Even
today he'll play-action teams to death."

Hearing my old quarterbacks say things like this makes
me realize one thing: I wouldn't trade my career for anybody's.
Not anybody's.

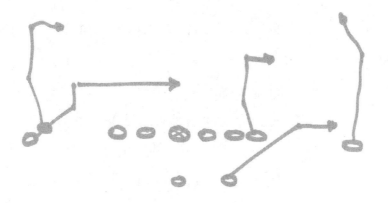

Bruce is the master when it comes to play calling. He has this uncanny ability to know what to call at just the perfect time. He also puts a lot of play-calling responsibility on his quarterbacks. He lets you pick your favorite plays. And this is really important: He listens to you during the game and is open to suggestions. Not many coaches will do that. But there's not many like Bruce in the NFL.

— BEN ROETHLISBERGER

CHAPTER 5

PLAY CALLING

My playbook? It's as thick as an old-fashioned big-city phone book, brother. It has descriptions and sketches of about 300 plays with notes on when in a game to use each one. I've built it over the course of thirty years and I'll use about a third of the plays in any given game.

The pass plays in my playbook consist of nine basic patterns, which can be considered the core principles of my aerial attack. The pass patterns are:

1. CURL

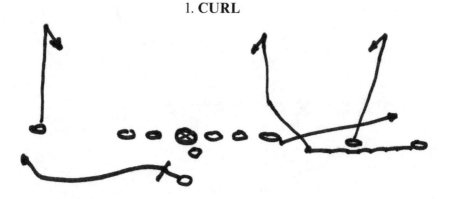

2. LOAD

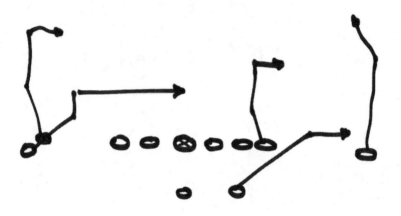

3. PIN

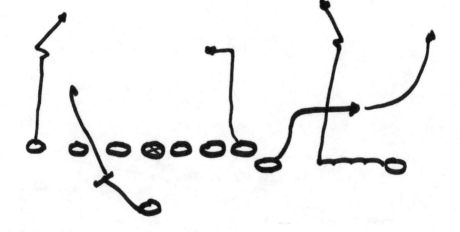

4. DIVIDE

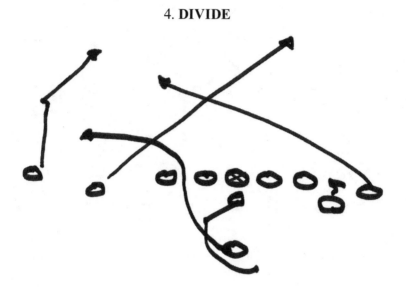

5. X-RAY

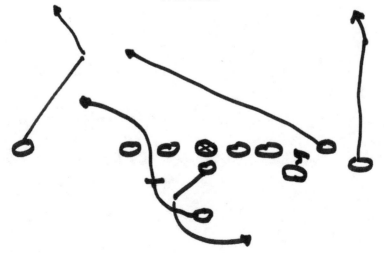

6. GO

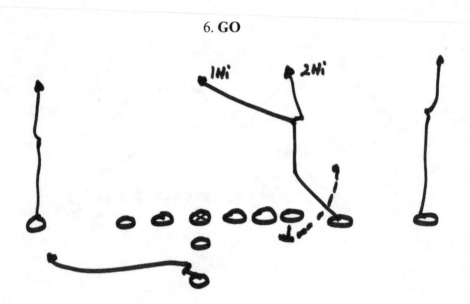

7. SLANT

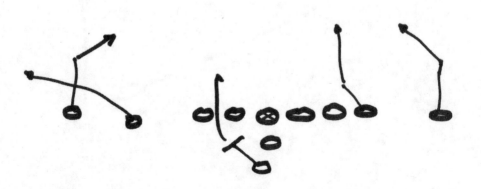

8. HITCH

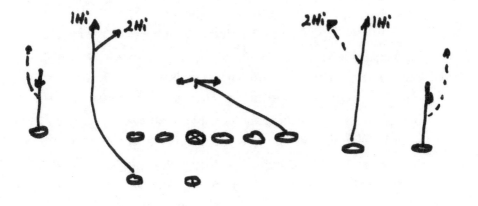

9. JET

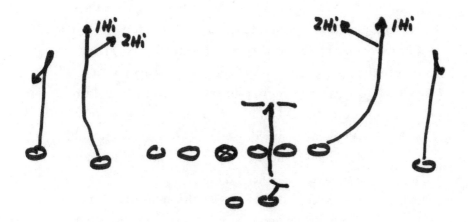

These nine routes literally contain hundreds of variations. The curl, for instance, can be run twenty-five different ways. So when putting together a game plan, I tweak the routes week to week. You always want to make sure that whatever your opponent believes you'll run and has been preparing to defend on game day, they aren't actually going to see once the opening whistle blows. This cat-and-mouse game between play callers and defensive coordinators never ends in the NFL.

My quarterback operates on a read-rotation system. At the line of scrimmage he'll diagnose the defense, and, based on what he sees, he'll decide who will be his number one option receiver. If, for example, there are two deep safeties lined up in the middle of the field, he'll know to attack the perimeter of the defense near the sidelines. If the defense lines up heavy on the strong side of the field—the strong side is the side where the tight end is lined up, usually to the right of the quarterback—the quarterback needs to immediately look to the weak side.

Then, as the QB drops back to pass, he works through his progressions, looking first at the best option, then the second best, and so on—what we call a read rotation. My whole offense is based on receivers beating their defenders in one-on-one situations. If the receiver does that and the quarterback has time to make an accurate throw, every pass should be a completion every time. And by God I mean, *every single time.*

My favorite play is called "88 Go." We employ maximum protection for the quarterback and then I'll send three guys deep, one down each sideline and one down the middle of the field. If all three receivers are covered, the quarterback has the flexibility to check down and throw to a running back flaring out of the backfield. I want a touchdown or a checkdown—the easy throw to the running back—with this play. But even this play has a run option for our quarterback built into it. If the coverage doesn't favor us, then at the line of scrimmage the quarterback should check to a run play.

"It's not just everybody runs a 'Go' route with Bruce," Carson Palmer says. "There's something underneath the route for every possible coverage. Sometimes, based on the defense, you need to get the ball out of your hands quick and make the defense turn and chase. And Bruce's offense gives the quarterback that flexibility. But the quarterback really has to study and put in the hours to understand where Bruce wants you to go with the ball in every type of situation that the defense will put you in."

Make no mistake: A successful offense is two-dimensional. It is fundamental in the NFL to run the ball. Ideally, I like to stay 50/50 in terms of passes and runs in a game. But the key is you have to surprise the defense, so we'll often line up in obvious running formations—like three tight ends—and throw it. We'll also line up in obvious passing formations—three wide receivers split out wide—and run a draw play. You always need to keep the other side guessing and off balance. You want them playing off their heels, not the balls of their feet.

When designing a game plan, it's important to self-scout and really be mindful of your own play calling. You don't want to tip your hand or establish a pattern or develop tendencies for certain down-and-distance situations where you're always calling the same play. So my staff and I are always reviewing our play calls of the previous two months and making sure we're not repeating ourselves and falling into any sort of pattern of play calls that an opposing defensive staff could pick up on. Every week we'll alter formations, we'll line up receivers in different spots, and we might add a few trick plays. Variation is key in the NFL. We're always looking for new ways to create mismatches for our best players. You always want your opponent to react to you—make him the puppet on your string—not the other way around.

I'll also incorporate a few new plays into the playbook each week. I want to throw things at defenses that they not only won't anticipate but also can't prepare for and practice on Wednesday and Thursday before games. The ideas for new plays can come from anywhere. A few years ago I was watching a small-college game on television when I saw an offensive play that I thought would never work. They were in the red zone and the quarterback faked a toss to his running back, then bootlegged to his right. All the linemen were pulling like it was running play to the left, so the quarterback was out there alone, a man on an island, fully exposed. In the red zone, defenses are very aggressive, and I was certain this quarterback was going to get flattened. But just before he got hit, he stopped, planted his feet, and arced a screen pass to his running back on the opposite side of the field. His back waltzed untouched into the end zone.

I'd never seen that play run before, but decided to give it a try out at practice one Friday when I was the interim head coach for the Colts in 2012. I was amazed: We scored a touchdown. Our entire offense practically doubled over in surprised shock. They were as amazed as I was that it worked.

The next week we were in overtime at Tennessee, the game tied at 13. We had the ball on the Titans' 16-yard line and it was second-and-10. I went with my gut and called that play I had seen the small-college run, even though we had only practiced it twice on Friday, which was the first time the players had ever heard of this play. There was no reason to call the play other than I thought it would work. No risk it, no biscuit.

Andrew Luck faked a pitch to Vick Ballard, then ran to his right. All of our linemen pulled left. Andrew threw the ball over a Tennessee defensive lineman—it cleared the lineman's hand by about an inch—and Vick caught it cleanly, unopposed, and scored a touchdown to end the game. We won 19–13. Our players went crazy. Man, as a coach, those are the sweetest moments; you just don't forget 'em.

I'll make about five or six gut calls a game. And they are rooted in feeling, in sensing how the game is unfolding and recalling something from memory that could work. The gut calls aren't on the play call script, but we'll have practiced them enough so our players will know how to execute the "feel" calls that I'll make.

In my view, play calling is an art form. You scout and research the tendencies of opposing defensive coordinators for hours on end. But they are aware of that, and they'll often throw wrinkles into their defensive schemes that they've never shown before. That's where the gut comes in. It's the ultimate chess match, a battle of brains. That's what makes coaching so damn fun.

* * *

Coaching can be heartbreaking as well. To this day, I can't set foot in the state of Alabama without being reminded of a gut call I made in the 1997 Iron Bowl between Alabama and Auburn. That was the day the trajectory of my career changed, the day that fundamentally altered my life—both personally and professionally. But looking back, I now consider it one of the best days of my career.

I was the offensive coordinator at Alabama, my second stint with the Crimson Tide coaching staff. We'd had a lousy season. Heading into our game with Auburn, we were 4–6 and obviously weren't going to be playing in a bowl game. The Tigers, conversely, were 8–2 and ranked thirteenth in the nation. So the only way to salvage our year was to beat Auburn in the blood feud that is the Iron Bowl, a rivalry between the state's largest two schools that dates back to 1893.

It's hard to overstate the importance of this game to the people of Alabama. What makes the annual Alabama–Auburn game so unique is that fans of the teams grow up with each other, go to high school with each other, work together, socialize together, go to church together, go hunting together, and, in many cases, get married. And whenever a conversation stalls at the office cooler, at a local barbecue pit, or at a neighborhood bar, there is always one fallback topic that you can damn well guarantee will be discussed: Which team is better, Alabama or Auburn? College football fans might be the most intense in all of American sports, and it's been my experience that the most zealous of those live in Alabama, where so much of the state's identity is tied to its two elite college football teams. It's repeatedly said that the state's most recognizable figures are: (1) the Alabama coach; (2) the Auburn coach; (3) the Crimson Tide starting quarterback; (4) the Auburn starting quarterback; and (5) the governor, and he's usually—strike that, *always*—a distant fifth.

So in that highly charged environment we played the sixty-second edition of the Iron Bowl at Jordan-Hare Stadium in Auburn.

After falling behind 6–0 in the first quarter, we scored 17 consecutive points. Our Crimson-clad fans in the stadium were whipped into a boiling froth. With 2:55 left in the fourth quarter, we had a 17–15 lead and the ball on our 20-yard line. All we needed was a few first downs and we'd pull off one of the biggest upsets in Iron Bowl history.

I started calling running plays for our wonderful tailback, Shaun Alexander, who would go on to star for the Seattle Seahawks. On back-to-back runs Shaun gained 17 yards. I called Shaun's number again on first down from our 37. The Tiger defense stuffed it for a one-yard loss. Auburn called a timeout. Now 1:35 remained on the game clock.

On second down we again handed the ball to Shaun, who picked up three yards. It was now third-and-eight. I'm thinking if we get a first down, it's kneeldown time. Game over.

I'm up in the press box. The clock is ticking. I called down to the sideline, asking the coaches—specifically, head coach Mike Dubose—what everyone wanted to do. But I didn't get an answer. Not a soul said a damn word. Later Dubose would tell a reporter, "I should have been more involved in that situation." I had to laugh when I read that. Hell yes, he should have been more involved. The head coach is the ultimate decision maker on the team, and at the most critical point of our season, he opted for radio silence.

Which was fine with me. I live for these situations. No risk it, no biscuit.

I called a simple screen pass. Our quarterback, Freddie Kitchens, rolled to his right and then floated a perfect pass back to his left to fullback Ed Scissum in the flat. Our left guard made a perfect block. But our left tackle, who may have been the best player on our team, whiffed on his block. If he makes that block, Scissum runs for 50 yards and the game is over. But he didn't make the block. Scissum got hit hard by an Auburn defender and fumbled the ball.

Auburn recovered with 42 seconds left. The Tigers then hit a last-second field goal and we lost, 18–17.

Man, the Alabama fans hurled verbal bile at me like sharpened spears. They were so irate you'd have thought I was personally responsible for all the famines and droughts in world history. But it was the right call. Sure, we could have run the ball up the middle, punted, and forced Auburn to drive about 60 yards with one timeout against our very talented defense. But my job as the play caller is to make sure we *win* the game on offense, not lose the game on defense. I'll go to my grave believing it was absolutely the right call.

Four days after the Iron Bowl I was fired.

Greatest thing ever, as it turned out.

Friends of mine told me I should clean out my office in the dead of night to avoid the media. Hell no, I said. I was going to do it in the light of day and answer any question anyone had.

I brought Jake with me to the office to gather my things. He was nineteen and a kicker at the University of Alabama– Birmingham. I wanted him to see the hard side of coaching. I knew he was thinking about pursuing a coaching career one day—and I wasn't going to deter him from it—but he needed to understand that coaching can be a very challenging life.

So Jake and I put my notebooks, mementos, pictures, and books into cardboard boxes and loaded up the car in front of the media. I answered all the questions with my chin held high. No, I told every reporter, I did not regret the play call. Sometimes in football plays don't work out the way they are designed, it was as simple as that.

A few weeks later, as I was sitting in my new house and wondering what in the world I was going to do with my life, I received a phone call from Jim Mora, the head coach of the Colts. He wanted to know if I would be interested in becoming his quarterback coach.

He also mentioned that the Colts had the first pick in the upcoming NFL draft, and they were thinking about selecting a kid out of the University of Tennessee. He asked me if I knew anything about Peyton Manning.

Yes, I did, I said. I mentioned that Peyton had recently torched us at Alabama for 304 yards passing and three touch- downs to lead the Vols to a 38–21 victory over us. I knew him well. Very well.

One door closes, another one opens.

And this was one heck of a door, because it turned out Peyton Manning would be standing on the other side. My football life was about to get very, very interesting.

* * *

My family life would never be the same either.

One of the main reasons why I took the job in Tuscaloosa was because I wanted my daughter, Kristi, to be in a college town. I had moved my family sixteen times and I wanted Kristi, who was a junior in high school when we moved to Alabama, to be able to finish high school in T-Town, as natives call Tuscaloosa. I genuinely thought I'd be the Crimson Tide's offensive coordinator for years.

It always was hard selling the moves to my kids, especially Kristi. Before each move I would usually walk into her bedroom and we'd sit on the bed together for a father-daughter talk. I'd tell Kristi that she was now going to have the chance to make more friends in a new city. "Some people grow up on the same street and never move," I said. "They only have two friends. Now you get to have a whole new set of friends. You'll have more friends than any young girl in America."

But the first days of school always terrified my daughter, and that always broke my heart into a million little pieces. It's tough to make friends when you're the outsider. I told her to be herself and that she'd have no problem winning over others. And she always would, but then we would move again the next year. And she'd be right back in the same boat and have to endure the trauma of another first day at school.

There were tears on every first day, but after about a week Kristi would usually find her comfort zone in the new school. Yet when we went to Alabama I promised her that this would be different. I swore to her she would finish high school in Tuscaloosa. So my wife and Kristi ended up staying in Alabama and I moved to Indianapolis by myself—the only time in my career I wasn't with my family. That, in a word, sucked. Big time.

But Kristi graduated from high school and then went to Alabama on a Bear Bryant Scholarship, which is a scholarship fund for the children of Alabama players and coaches. So all those years after I sat in Coach Bryant's office and said goodbye to him a final time, he was back in my life, paying for my daughter's education.

Talk about a legacy.

But these really hard times strengthened her character and made her the strong woman she is today. My bond with my little girl remains as powerful as ever.

In the NFL, if we have a game on Sunday, then Monday will be evaluation day. The entire team will be in the facility watching the just-over game with their position coaches. We'll review, in painstaking detail, what went right, what went wrong, and how we can improve.

The players have Tuesday off. But for the coaches, it's game plan day for our upcoming opponent. We'll arrive in the office early and brainstorm for hours. By the end of this marathon meeting, we'll have a clear idea of what we want to do on offense, defense, and special teams. We have a big whiteboard covering an entire wall in our coaches' conference room, and we'll write every play of the game plan on that board. But the plays on the whiteboard are always works in progress during the week—the board seems to contain dozens and dozens of living, breathing organisms—because we'll constantly tweak the game plan, adding and subtracting a few plays as we get closer to kickoff.

The quarterbacks only get *most* of Tuesday off. By 8 p.m. that night we'll email the quarterbacks the game plan, which will pop up on their tablets. Carson Palmer loves to devour the game plan that very evening. A longtime NFL veteran, Carson understands that he needs to know our plan of attack better than anyone who's not a coach. So during the 2016 season, after reading a bedtime story to his seven-year-old twins, Fletch and Ellie, he'd plop down in his office at home that sits in the shadow of Camelback Mountain and begin his work for the week. It can't be stressed enough: Physical ability, which Carson has in spades, means very little in the NFL if your mental skills aren't as robust and as finely tuned. Carson usually spends about two hours studying every Tuesday night before Sunday games.

There is a lot for the quarterbacks to learn. Sometimes I'll include as many as 150 plays in the game plan. Not only does the QB need to know the precise contours of each play, but he needs to know the formation for each play, the personnel combination for each play, and what defensive formations he's likely to see for each play. Then he needs to think about what he would change to if the defense lines up in a formation we're not expecting. If that change is to a pass, he needs to know the progressions for the new pass play. And if the change is to a run, he needs to know the proper call based on what he views as the most vulnerable point of that defensive alignment that we weren't anticipating in the first place. No, it ain't easy being an NFL quarterback.

Wednesdays are installation days. We'll review the game plan in position meetings in the morning. Then, in the afternoon, out on the practice field, we'll methodically go through the twenty-five third-down plays and the thirty-five first-down plays that we plan to run in the game.

On Thursdays we'll practice red-zone plays and the two-minute drill. We'll show the players what has occurred to our upcoming opponent in the red zone and in two-minute situations in their previous few games—both the good and the bad—so we can learn them and hopefully exploit their weaknesses on game day.

The most important part of my week happens on Thursday mornings. Alone in my office, I'll analyze every morsel, every bit of information at my disposal. This can take hours, but I think games can be won and lost during this time. I'll come up with my top thirty offensive plays that I'll want to run in the game. I'll then write them on our big whiteboard in the main coaches' conference room. I'll always get this done by late afternoon. Why? Because Thursday nights are also key for me: That's date night with Chris. It's basically the only time of the week it's just the two of us, which is why it's so special.

Friday practices are dedicated to short-yardage situations and goal-line plays with blitzes. After practice the quarterbacks and I will head back into our conference room with the whiteboard. I pick the first fifteen running plays we'll call in the game, but I leave it to our starting quarterback to select the first fifteen pass plays.

I want my quarterback to feel—to believe—he's got a key role in shaping the game plan. I also want to raise his level of accountability. So once we're in the meeting room, Carson will walk up to the whiteboard and mark his favorite fifteen pass plays. I never want to call a pass a quarterback is not comfortable with. After we discuss those plays, Carson will circle his four favorites. These will be our first four pass plays of the game. This entire process takes about an hour.

Coaches have been scripting the opening plays of games since Bill Walsh started doing that in the late 1970s. Bill's sheet had fifteen plays on it. I script my first thirty. In those plays I try to get each guy involved. I want our running backs to have a few carries and begin to get a feel for the game. I want all of our wide receivers to have a chance to make a catch or two. The earlier your best players are engaged in the game, the better they'll generally play for the remainder of it. That's why the first thirty offensive plays are so extremely important.

I always try to put each player on my team in the best possible position to be successful. This is what coaching is all about, but it's not always easy. When I arrived in Arizona in 2013, Larry Fitzgerald—the most popular player in franchise history and a first-ballot Hall of Famer—was struggling playing our X position, which is split end (the receiver who is usually lined up farthest to the outside). He had lost a little speed and I thought he needed to learn how to play the slot position, the inside receiving spot. Plus, if he moved inside, it would be much more difficult for opponents to double-team Larry and basically take him out of the game.

I explained to Larry that I helped Reggie Wayne make a position transition in Indianapolis and Hines Ward do the same in Pittsburgh. It extended both of their careers. Let's face it: Larry was thirty years old, and thirty-year-old wide receivers tend to lose a step. If he wanted to keep producing at a high level, I believed his best position was the slot. But when I told Larry this he looked at me like a kid who had only eaten ice cream all his life and was now being forced to try spinach. "Just call Reggie and Hines and ask them how their position changes worked out," I said to him. "You're going to still get the football if you move inside. You can do it."

At first Larry really was lost. He slowed down pass patterns because, after years of playing outside, he wasn't totally comfortable and certain where to go. He struggled reading the middle of the field—he had trouble figuring out whether the defenses were in man or zone coverage—and often didn't know if he should hook in or cut to the outside. I told him, "You should have seen Reggie Wayne when I flipped him over to the right side. The guy couldn't stop tripping over his feet, because Reggie had played left wide receiver his entire career. But he worked at it and he got better. You can do the same thing."

Larry bought in—he's a pro's pro—and gradually improved. But then in 2015, I had a new idea for him: Let's make him our Z. The Z is the wide receiver who lines up outside but motions inside before the ball is snapped. "I want you on the move," I told him. "You won't get pressed man-to-man and you'll get more balls thrown your way. You'll have to block more, but if you do that, I'll reward you with red-zone plays."

Man, now Larry really bought in. In 2015 I think he was the best blocking receiver in the NFL. That was why our running game got so much better. In '14 we were thirty-first in the league in rushing; the next year, with Larry blocking from the Z position, we jumped to eighth in the NFL in rushing and our average rush went from 3.3 yards per play to 4.2.

Plus, it became harder for the defense to keep track of Larry and focus their coverage on him. He could line up all over the field, and if we wanted, he could motion back and forth as Carson called out the cadence.

It worked just as I had hoped: At age thirty-two in 2015, Larry caught a career-high 109 passes. And just as I had promised him, he was our first look in the red zone on play-action passes. He wound up with nine touchdown receptions. We had put him, I believe, in the best position possible to flourish—and he sure did.

He was brilliant in 2016 as well. He caught 107 balls for 1,023 yards. At age thirty-three, my man Fitz led the NFL in receptions and was selected to his tenth Pro Bowl—among wide receivers, only Jerry Rice has been to more.

On Saturday nights I meet one final time with my quarterbacks in the team hotel. We usually have chapel at 7:30 and then I'll sit down with my guys at 8 p.m. for about thirty minutes. This is the chance for my starting QB to tell me his preferences for all the different types of situations and scenarios we'll be in during the game. I listen very closely to his every word and pay close attention to his demeanor. If I sense that he feels overwhelmed or has some lingering doubts in his mind, I extend the meeting.

"I always want more time with B.A. on Saturday nights,"

Carson says. "I'll usually come up with about fifteen questions ahead of our meeting, and then I'll try to figure out which of those are the dumbest and get rid of them. I'll usually ask like three or four questions that I really need answers to. This is a very important time in our game week."

Game day is showtime—the best day of the week. If we're playing at home here in Arizona, we usually have a house full of family and friends staying with us and we'll get up early for breakfast. I'll shower, kiss my wife, and then my assistant, Wesley Goodwin, will pick me up. We'll arrive at the stadium about three hours before kickoff.

I'll greet the stadium workers, which is so much fun. There are usually military personnel around our locker room and out on the field, so I'll thank them for their service and take a bunch of pictures with them. This is a very relaxing time for me, because I know I've done everything I can to be prepared for the game. We may not win, but it sure as hell won't be for lack of effort.

I'll then head into my office in the stadium for a little quiet time. I'll flip on a few of the East Coast NFL games and watch for a few minutes. That's one of the great things about being in the Southwest—the NFL action east of the Mississippi starts hours before our games. As a fan and as a coach, I love it. We get football virtually all day in the desert.

Then one of my assistants will give me a warning that the officials are about to come talk to me. I'll put a fake smile on my face and try to sweet-talk them for as long as they'll listen.

After that I'll walk into the locker room to look into the eyes of my players. Our Cardinals teams have always had very loose, loud locker rooms. I let our guys listen to music and they love it.

I'll wander out onto the field and watch our quarterbacks throw their warm-up tosses. I always pay very close attention to Carson, making sure his tempo and balance are proper. If he struggles with a particular throw, I'll make him repeat it until he and I are comfortable with it. You want to get everything right just before the game, and I certainly don't want Carson questioning himself when he has to make that throw in the game.

As kickoff nears, we'll gather in the locker room. I'll have one of the players say a prayer. Then I'll tell the team in a confident, steady voice something challenging like, "Let's play the best thirty minutes of football we've ever played."

I'll then walk at the head of the mass of my players toward the tunnel. They'll wait at its mouth while I'll go stand near the 50-yard line. The players will charge out onto the field and I'll look up into the head coach's box and see Chris, the love of my life. I always blow her a kiss; she blows one, sometimes two, back.

Game time is anxiously close now. We'll stand on the sideline as the national anthem is played. After all these years, after literally hearing those notes thousands of times, I still get a tear in my eye when I hear "the rockets' red glare."

The anthem, the roar of the crowd, the rising excitement in the stadium signal the approaching time—the time for a football game. It's the greatest three hours in sports, a span of time when a bunch of grown-up kids get to play a game for a living.

God, America really is great!

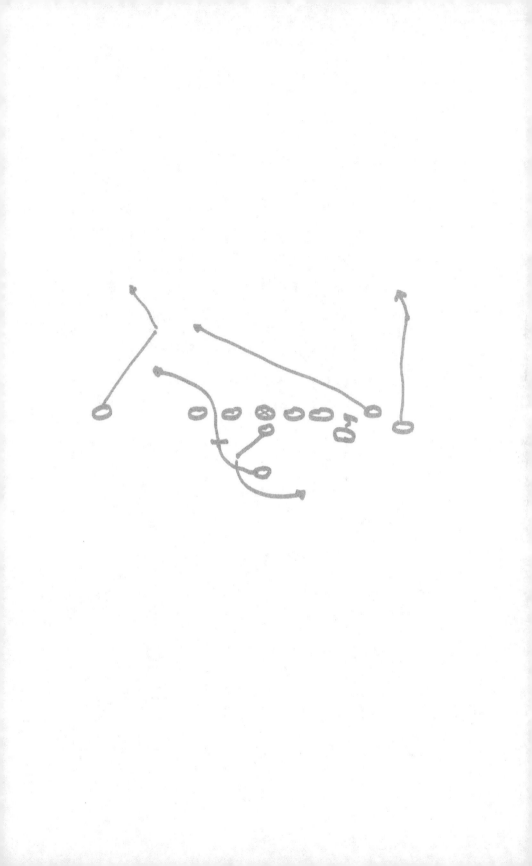

Bruce is definitely like a cool uncle to his quarterbacks. He's all work on the field, but away from football you can play a round of golf with and just hang out with him. He's easy to talk to and he truly cares about his quarterbacks. .

— BEN ROETHLISBERGER

CHAPTER 6

BEN ROETHLISBERGER

Before the 2004 draft, when I was the wide receivers coach with the Steelers, I ranked the prominent quarterbacks who were about to come out of the collegiate ranks, from Eli Manning to Philip Rivers to Ben Roethlisberger. In my judgment it was a no-brainer who the best NFL player of the three was going to be—Big Ben.

At Miami (Ohio) University he was a very special player, showing that rare twin trait of avoiding onrushing linemen while simultaneously keeping his eyes downfield. Too often the so-called draft experts who have never coached or played a down in the NFL just focus on the physical traits of college quarterbacks. They ask questions such as: *Does he have the prototypical size? Can he make all the necessary throws? Is he agile, quick afoot, fast?* But I like to see if the guy can keep his eyes down the field in the midst of mounting chaos. Is he a leader and winner? In short, does he have grit? Ben checked off those boxes.

We had Tommy Maddox as our starting QB and we were all set to draft Shawn Andrews, a mountain of an offensive tackle out of Arkansas. We held the eleventh overall pick and we thought all the top quarterbacks—Ben, Eli, and Philip—would be off the board when it came time for us to make a selection.

But then we couldn't believe our luck. While Eli had gone first to the Chargers and Rivers fourth to the Giants (they would soon be traded for each other), Ben had slid down the draft board because teams had needs other than quarterback, and he was available when it was our pick. When asked, I weighed in with my two cents, telling everyone in our windowless war room in Pittsburgh that Ben had all the tools—mental and physical—to be a star.

We selected Big Ben. The Steelers franchise would have its face for the next decade-plus. But man, I had no idea what a royal pain in the posterior Ben would briefly become for me.

The plan for Ben's rookie season was for him to hold a clipboard on the sideline and study, play by play, how our starter, Tommy Maddox, managed and played each game. In a perfect world, it's best not to play rookie quarterbacks. The NFL game is so much faster than the college game, and the NFL's defensive schemes are so much more complex than those faced by college QBs. I tell my young quarterbacks to take mental reps during games—visualize that they are out on the field and react to everything the opposing defense throws at our starter. Still, there is no substitute for being out on the field in live action, in the line of withering fire.

In our second game of Ben's rookie year we faced the Baltimore Ravens. Again, our plan for the year was to keep Ben on the bench or only play sparingly. We knew he was our future franchise quarterback—we'd already seen in pre-season that he had the potential to be very, very special—and we didn't want to hamper his development by throwing him into the cauldron before he was ready. I've seen several young QBs forced to play before they were ready—Akili Smith in Cincinnati and David Carr in Houston, for example—and had their confidence obliterated, killing their careers. We wanted to save Ben from that potential fate. But in the third quarter against the Ravens, Tommy sprained his elbow when Baltimore defensive end Terrell Suggs hit him. Big Ben trotted out onto the field for his first regular-season action.

Using a relatively simple game plan against the Ravens, Ben led us on a mini-comeback. He threw fourth-quarter touchdown passes to Antwaan Randle El and Hines Ward. But he also threw two interceptions; Chris McAlister returned one 51 yards for a touchdown late in the game. We lost 30–13.

But I loved what Ben said to the media after the game. "I'm not Tommy Maddox," he told reporters. "Can't be Tommy Maddox. I'm just going to do the best that I can."

Tommy understood every nuance of our offense, and Ben was still learning its basics. So we certainly had to scale back the number of different things we did. Yet, even in his first NFL action, it was abundantly clear that the game wasn't too big for this 6'5", 240-pound rookie. He looked like he belonged on the field for one reason—he did.

The entire staff knew it. The next week we flew to Miami, where Ben made his first start. We landed only hours before Hurricane Jeanne blew through South Florida. While we were told that our team hotel was hurricane-proof, that night the electricity went out. Transformers blew up all around us. The hotel staff gave our players flashlights, and then something else happened out of the stormy blue—our team bonded together.

Guys ran through the halls and up and down stairwells playing flashlight tag like a bunch of twelve-year-olds on vacation. When a generator cranked up and pushed power to the kitchen, a group of players descended on it and gorged on ice cream. We all had a blast. "Chemistry" is an overused word. But that night our guys really began to care about each other. When you truly care about your teammates, you become accountable to them. Shared accountability, trust in one another, loyalty among one another creates unity of effort, teamwork—in short, a team.

The rain poured throughout the game, but Ben loved it— thrived in it like a big duck. In the fourth quarter he did what he always did: After completing two key third-down passes to Plaxico Burress and Hines Ward, he hit Hines on a seven-yard touchdown pass—the only touchdown of the game. We won 13–3.

We ended up going 13–0 in the regular season with a damn rookie as our starting quarterback. Fucking unbelievable. At the time the NFL record for most wins by a rookie starting at quarterback was six, held by Chris Chandler and Joe Ferguson. Ben vaporized that stat.

Ben had the body of a linebacker and yet he could run like a tight end. He was just so damn athletic. When you have a quarterback who can move around the pocket and extend plays, it adds a dimension to your offense that is very difficult to defend against because a defensive coordinator can't really prepare for it. Even from the perspective of the Pittsburgh coaching staff, sometimes it looked like Ben was out there making up plays like he was in some vacant-lot game, the way he scrambled around, pointed to where he wanted receivers to run, and would then just sling the ball all over the place. For us, he was fun to watch, even as we held our breath. As a young player he took far too many sacks, but that's because he genuinely believed he could evade danger, remain upright, and throw a touchdown pass on every play. That was how much confidence he had in his own ability.

Ben had an elite arm, no question. What separated him from so many others was his ability to pass with accuracy when on the move. So many times quarterbacks lose their ability to thread the needle once their feet start moving. But not Ben. He could be just as accurate running away from a 320-pound defensive lineman as he could standing statue-like in the pocket.

At Miami University he played in a spread formation that typically featured three or four wide receivers fanned out across the field. This was why we planned to sit him during his first season. We wanted to teach him the basics of our pro-style attack and get him comfortable taking snaps from under center.

But life in the NFL—just like life in the real world—rarely goes according to plan. So when Tommy went down with his elbow injury, we handed the keys to the offense to Ben. At first, we told him to drive the car at a slow rate of speed and not take any chances; just keep the wheels on the road. But then as we won game after game after game, we basically told him, "Okay, you've grown up before our eyes. The car is yours. Drive it as fast as you can without wrecking the thing."

Ben led us to the Super Bowl in his second year in the league. But inside the locker room it was hardly all rosy for him.

During the season Ben often acted immature, as if all the stories that documented the greatness of "Big Ben" had gone to his head. He wasn't signing as many autographs for team-mates as he should; some days he would sign, some days he wouldn't. Late in the season head coach Bill Cowher asked a few veterans to speak to the team before we played Detroit late in the season. At the time we needed to win our final five games to make the playoffs.

Hines Ward, Aaron Smith, Jerome Bettis, and Joey Porter addressed the team. Each guy talked about what we needed to do to win, and Joey zeroed in on Ben. Using blunt language, he told Ben that if he was going to be our leader, he needed to be "one of us." To his credit, Ben listened—though he didn't really have a choice. After that moment he became a different person. He grew up fast.

Everything changed for Ben. He started wooing his offensive line by taking them out to top-flight dinners and giving them meaningful gifts. He became the leader of our team, our Pied Piper. All young quarterbacks in the NFL have to grow up, but I don't think I've ever seen one mature as fast as Ben.

That all went back to Joey's advice to him.

On February 5, 2006, we faced the Seattle Seahawks in Super Bowl XL in Detroit. We were up 14–10 in the fourth quarter and moving the ball down the field when I mentioned to Ken Whisenhunt, our offensive coordinator and play caller, that a reverse pass would work. I had been analyzing the movements of the Seahawks defensive backs and was virtually dead certain that they would run toward the line of scrimmage at the moment they saw the reverse. Then, I believed, Hines Ward would be open on a deep pass. No risk it, no biscuit.

"If we make it to midfield with a first down I think we should call it," I told Wiz over the headset.

It's so important for every coach—and every player, for that matter—to know his particular role on the team and accept that role. During this season my role was to protect Ken Whisenhunt and make his job as easy as possible. So one of my main duties was to keep our starting wide receivers, Hines Ward and Plaxico Burress, off Ken's ass. Both Hines and Plaxico were strong-willed individuals, and they would get upset when they thought they weren't getting enough passes thrown their way. But I also made sure they vented to me, their receivers coach, and not to Ken, who was busy calling the game.

Earlier that season I had also talked to Bill Cowher about interfering with Ken's play calls. There were a few times early on when, over the headset, Bill would hear a play call by Ken and say something like, "Here comes a fumble." I eventually went into Bill's office and explained that the head coach can't undercut the confidence of the play caller. "Look, you got a young play caller calling plays for the first time," I said to him. "You don't want him calling plays to please you. You want him to call plays to beat the other team. I've heard you say 'Oh my God' on the headset after a play call. You can't do that. You need to concentrate on your job and Kenny needs to concentrate on his job."

"I really do that?" Bill asked.

"Yes, Coach," I said

After that, Bill kept his knee-jerk, oh-my-God thoughts to himself during games.

During the Super Bowl, after I told Ken my idea for the reverse pass, he agreed to call it. Even though it was the first time all season that we'd run the play, it worked to perfection: a reverse to wide receiver Antwaan Randle El, a former college quarterback at Indiana, who then threw the ball deep down the field to a wide open Hines Ward. Just as I suspected, the Seahawks safeties charged at Antwaan once he had the ball. Hines caught the pass for a 43-yard touchdown and we never looked back. We won 21–10. Ben, at age twenty-three, became the youngest quarterback ever to win a Super Bowl.

My parents had been with me the week of the game. They really enjoyed riding the elevator up and down with our players in the team hotel. I mean, they wouldn't get off it. They loved talking to players and having photos taken with them. A player came up to me during the week and said, "Hey, B.A., I just rode with your mom on the elevator." And I replied, "Is she still on that damn thing?"

As soon as the game was over, the confetti fell on us as world champions. I quickly looked up into the stands to find my parents. Our eyes eventually locked, and the smile on my dad's face was the most incredible thing I'd ever seen since the look he had a quarter century earlier when I was introduced at a Temple University press conference as the newly hired youngest head coach in the country. This topped that. It's like he finally knew that his son—the one who got kicked out of high school—had made his way in the world. I was aware enough to freeze that image of my beaming dad in my mind, because it was like my entire career and path in life had been vindicated and validated. All sons, no matter how old, want the approval of their fathers.

My dad was so important to me. I called him after every game. When I was the head coach at Temple and we beat Pittsburgh in 1984 for the first time in about forty-five years, he was in the stadium to witness it. He was always there for the special moments in my life.

After we won the Super Bowl, I took my mom and dad to our team party in the hotel outside Detroit. They were wearing Super Bowl Champion T-shirts and both had ear-to-ear grins on their faces. We eventually bumped into Bill Cowher. He leaned over and told my dad above the noise, "What a great call your son made. He's a hell of a coach."

My dad smiled brilliantly again.

That Super Bowl was the last game he ever saw me coach. He died of a heart attack a few months later at age seventy-nine. But those moments and experiences after that Super Bowl are something I'll always cherish, just seeing how proud my dad was. This is football at its best, bringing a son and father close, sharing a bonding experience that can be savored for a lifetime.

At my dad's funeral I put a little bottle of gin and two golf balls in his pocket as he lay in his coffin. He always carried two balls with him because he always wanted to be prepared to hit that mulligan. And that's really how life is—you always need to be ready to take another swing if your first shot doesn't work out the way you hoped it would.

The year after we won the Super Bowl, Ken Whisenhunt was hired to be the head coach of the Arizona Cardinals. I took Ken's place and became the Steelers' offensive coordinator. That meant that my relationship with Ben was about to change.

Ben and I did not always see eye to eye. He thought I had yelled at the receivers too much, and he told me so during one of our first meetings. "Dude, you're the quarterback, man," I replied. "I don't yell at QBs. I gotta yell at the knucklehead receivers! They won't listen if you don't."

Ben laughed, and that broke the ice. But I still didn't think he worked hard enough on his craft. Sure, we had just won the Super Bowl, but Ben's fundamentals—such as his footwork and simple things like running out a handoff by acting like he still had the ball—still weren't as good as I felt they should be. Plus his stroke needed some work. In his first two years he had a great defense behind him and basically he just had to win third downs. Now I wanted to make him into a complete quarterback.

Ben and I had never taken the time to get to know each other on a personal level. To change that, I played golf with him at Treesdale, a country club in Pittsburgh. Later, I invited him to our new club in Reynolds Plantation, Georgia.

I like to think that I can get along with everybody, that I'm as easygoing as a Sunday afternoon drive. In 1970, Virginia Tech assistant coach John Devlin handpicked me to become the first white player to room with a black player in school history. I didn't think twice about breaking this segregation barrier; my closest friends in my old neighborhood in York were black. I was the quarterback on our Pee Wee football team—I had snow-white hair and was one of the few Caucasian kids on the roster—and the mothers of the black players called me "Whitey." I thought it was hilarious.

At Tech I became fast friends with my new roommate, James Barber; we hung a sign on our dorm-room door that read "Salt and Pepper Inc." We wore each other's clothes and hit it off as if we'd known each other for years. A few times white players would come by and ask me, "What's it like living with a black guy?" I'd roll my eyes and shoot back, "I'm sure it's a hell of a lot better than living with you. Your shit is dirty all the time and James is the greatest guy in the world."

"You've got to remember that this was Virginia Tech and there's a lot of southern kids," Chris says. "The coaches were looking around and saw Bruce, this Yankee guy who seemed really cool and got along with everyone. Bruce grew up in an integrated neighborhood and he's never thought anything about color. It's still that way today. It doesn't even enter into the equation."

James and I became graduate assistants together at Virginia Tech. We grew so close that Chris and I babysat James's twin boys, Ronde and Tiki—future NFL stars. Tiki was sick a lot as a kid—he had fevers and convulsions—and so Chris and I would take care of Ronde when the family was at the hospital with Tiki. I'll never forget bouncing Ronde on my knee for hours. Even today, I get a big kick out of hugging those Barber twins.

"Bruce can talk street with anyone, and if he needs to, he can be the most intellectual guy in the room," New York Jets head coach Todd Bowles says. Todd played for me at Temple in the mid-1980s and he was my defensive coordinator at Arizona in 2013 and '14. "Because of Bruce's unique background, he can reach absolutely everyone on a football roster," Todd says, "and that's the key to building chemistry and building a winning team."

I knew the key to reaching Ben was winning his trust—just like I had won the trust of James Barber back at Tech. As always, I did my background research on Ben.

Ben's parents divorced when he was two. He lived with his father, Ken. When he was eight he was shooting baskets in his driveway as he waited for his mother, Ida, to pick him up for her visit. But his mom never arrived. She was involved in a crash with a pickup truck and later passed away due to her injuries.

But Ben grew up in a loving family in Findlay, a town of about 37,000 in northwest Ohio. He called his stepmother "Mom." His dad, a former pitcher and quarterback at Georgia Tech, helped him excel at sports. The people I spoke to said that in junior high Ben would shoot baskets for hours on end at his local rec center. He grew into a fabulous multisport athlete; he excelled in football, basketball, and baseball. Remember, that is typically a key to the development of a young quarterback, a predictor of his success.

Ben was something of a leader as well. He didn't drink booze in high school, and when he was at high school parties and the police were called due to a noise complaint, he typically was the one chosen by the crowd to speak to the arriving officers. On the field as a senior he was a sight to see. He threw 54 touchdown passes, including eight in one game, and passed for more than 4,100 yards. It was easy to see that this kid possessed the raw tools to become a future successful NFL quarterback.

Everyone I chatted with described Ben as an intense competitor; whether he was playing a game of H-O-R-S-E or table tennis or pool, he was exceedingly driven to win. That is another hallmark characteristic that most future NFL quarterbacks display as young men.

But I do think Ben had trouble letting people get close to him. One exception was when he played at Miami of Ohio and he became extremely tight with head coach Terry Hoeppner. Coach Hoeppner created a family atmosphere in his program—his grandchildren often attended practice—and Ben grew to consider him like a second father. I know Ben took it very hard when Coach Hoeppner died in 2007 from complications of a brain tumor. It was as if Ben had again lost a parent.

Coach Hoeppner meant everything to Ben. They met in the summer of 1999 after Ben had finished his junior year at Findlay High in Ohio. Ben had spent that season as a receiver at the varsity squad—the coach's son was the quarterback—but at a football camp Hoeppner spotted Ben throwing passes and quickly realized that the kid had arm talent. Ben had played quarterback on the jayvee team at Findlay, but he didn't start on varsity until his senior season. He threw six touchdown passes in his first game, and that was enough for Hoeppner to offer him a scholarship. Ohio State later recruited Ben, but by then it was too late: He had committed to play for Hoeppner. And this is the thing about Ben—he's a man of his word.

Ben left Miami of Ohio after his junior year. Coach Hoeppner went with him to the draft in New York City. The two were so close that Ben would call him every Friday night before our games on Sunday. So I knew there was a big void in Ben's life after Coach Hoeppner passed away.

But I never want to be a father figure to my quarterbacks. I've got my own kids. I want to be the cool uncle you'd like to have a drink with, the guy you can spill your guts to without fearing reprisal. And that's what I told Ben shortly after I became his offensive coordinator.

Once Ben was on the golf course with me at Reynolds Plantation, on Lake Oconee eighty miles east of Atlanta, I calmly started talking to him, man to man. For a few hours we drank cold beer—we both enjoy doing that—and we swung the sticks. We got to know each other.

I told Ben about my own rebellious streak, explaining how I'd been kicked out of York Catholic High as a senior after I'd been caught swilling beer with a few of my football buddies. I felt that I had been unfairly singled out—thirty players went on a retreat; twenty-nine got suspended for three days and one got booted from school—but that was the hand I had been dealt.

But that incident was a turning point for me. Before then, I had never really thought about what distant horizons might have in store for me. I knew I didn't want to be a welder—I worked that job one summer and it was as hard as shit—but I didn't have a clear idea of what I wanted to do with my life. This changed the moment I saw the disappointment on my dad's face when we were told I was being expelled from school. Because from that instant forward, I finally realized what had to be my life's mission: to win back the honor of my family name. I still didn't know exactly what I was going to do, but damn it, I was determined to become a success.

After I was shown the door at York Catholic High, every college that had been recruiting me to play football suddenly quit calling—except for Virginia Tech. The only reason Tech stayed with me, I told Big Ben, was because the assistant who was recruiting me told the rest of the Hokie staff that I switched schools simply to take a more advanced math class at the public school. What a joke that was—the idea of me taking any type of advanced math class was as preposterous as finding candy on the moon—but that little white lie, which you could get away with in those pre-Internet days, allowed me to go to Tech. That act of kindness by Tech coach John Devlin also solidified my belief in giving people second chances, which is why, years later, I decided to pick Tyrann Mathieu in the third round of the 2013 draft after he had been kicked out of LSU for his well-documented drug problem. I got to know Tyrann before the draft and I knew his heart. He was a good kid who owned up to his mistakes and was committed to being a professional football player. Since he's been with us, Tyrann has been a big asset to the Cardinals, both on and off the field.

After a day of golf at Reynolds Plantation, Ben and I crashed into big comfortable chairs on my porch. As the descending sun bled red-gold across the horizon, I told Ben—yes, of course, each of us had a cocktail in our hands—that I wanted him to help me rewrite the playbook. I said, "If you show me you can handle it, I'll let you call the plays."

Ben was thrilled, nearly falling out of his chair. But that proposition was crucial to the future. I needed him to take ownership of the offense, and his response was just what I hoped it would be. I now knew that he was going to take his game, and our team, to the next level.

Ben spent hours and hours editing the playbook. He got rid of some plays, added a few, and even renamed some. It was important for him to develop terminology that was easy for him to remember and convey to his teammates in the huddle. So we shortened a few things. For instance, a "Post In Comeback" route became PIC.

When we later gathered for the first practices of the upcoming season, Ben was more serious, more dedicated to his craft. He had been used to getting the game plan when he arrived at the facility on Wednesday before our Sunday game, but now he was going to be by my side on Tuesday in my office helping me to create the plan. Ben couldn't get enough football. We were now tethered at the hip—the way it should be with a quarterback coach and his starting QB—and we would either succeed or fail together. Ben knew that I was going to fight for him and stick by him, and in return he began working his ass off. He refined his throwing motion. He focused on his footwork. Every day at practice it was like he was preparing to play in the next Super Bowl.

Because I had given him ownership of the offense, he now felt personally invested in it. He became a great practice player—a far cry from his first two years in the league, when he sometimes would just go through the motions and let his mind wander. And the guys on the team saw this transformation in him as well. Day by day, practice by practice, Ben started to become the leader of the team, leading by his actions.

"Bruce and I built our communication on the golf course," Ben says. "I even bought a house down there in Reynolds Plantation to be close to Bruce. He showed that he trusted me, and I busted my tail to reward that trust."

In training camp Ben played at the highest level of his career. He went a dozen practices without throwing a single interception. By the time the first regular-season game rolled around, at Cleveland, he was so comfortable with the playbook that I gave him the freedom to change plays at the line of scrimmage. For the first time in his career, he also called the offensive line protections based on how the defense lined up. Against the Browns, Ben threw four touchdown passes in our 34–7 victory.

That was just a sample of what was to come. For the first time since I'd been with him, it seemed like Ben couldn't get enough of football. We talked plays, formations, and philosophy over lunch and in my office at all hours. He was always thinking about different ways to attack different defenses. In the process, he also took his leadership to a new level. He started shaking hands with every player during pregame warm-ups and became a vocal presence on the sideline. In short, he was growing up before my eyes.

In my first season as Pittsburgh's offensive coordinator, with my quarterback calling some of his own plays, Ben compiled a passer rating of 104.1, still the best of his career. That season, 2007, he played in his first Pro Bowl.

But it wasn't until 2008 that I felt we really began to click to the point that we could almost read each other's minds— even though I continually had to remind him that he wasn't Superman out there on the field. "Ben, every play is not designed to score a touchdown," I repeatedly told him. "Sometimes you just have to take what the defense gives you and throw the underneath route." But Ben could be hardheaded. He got hurt twice that season by holding on to the ball too long and taking big hits.

Ben is as tough as they come. I've seen him play with so many injuries over the years and never complain to his teammates or the media. There were times when he could barely move his legs. Against Baltimore in '08 he was so immobile that we put him in the pistol formation—he lined up four yards behind center—the entire game; he insisted he didn't want to be taken out. My advice to him that day was simple—protect yourself by getting the ball out of your hands as quickly as possible. Operating entirely from the pocket, he led us to a 13–9 come-from-behind victory, completing 22 of 40 passes for 246 yards. It was one of the gutsiest performances I'd ever witnessed.

That afternoon his teammates could see he was hurting, and that earned him even more respect in the locker room. When the leader of your team is also the toughest player on your team, that's an ideal situation. Fair or not, the other players on both sides of the ball follow the lead of the quarterback. And when Ben grits his teeth and plays through pain, it inspires other players to do the same. It's almost impossible to overstate the value of that for any NFL team.

We went 12–4 in the 2008 regular season, winning six games at Heinz Field. After each of those victories, the coaches and the players always knew where the party was going to be held— the back of my car.

I work hard, but I also play hard. Everyone needs balance in life. And so after a win in our yard that season, I'd shower, change, do any interviews if reporters wanted to talk to me, and then head for my car parked in the players' and coaches' lot. I'd pop open the trunk and would have a few coolers chock full of drinks on ice: beers, bourbon, vodka. You name it, I had it. Hey, once a bartender, always a bartender.

I'm a Crown Royal sipper. Once I got to the car, I'd pour a drink for myself and then start pouring more for the players and coaches who gathered around my ride. These little post-game parties were some of my happiest times in Pittsburgh—I still throw them in our parking lot in Arizona—because for an hour or two we can relax and enjoy each other as friends, not coworkers or teammates, just pals. I loved it. Players and coaches brought their families over. We were just like everyone else who tailgated in parking lots after the games—friends and family enjoying each other's company.

Hell, truth be told, even if we didn't win, we'd still tailgate. I admit, those parties after a loss weren't as joyful and didn't last as long, but we still had a good time. I like to believe that I never lost a parking-lot tailgate, the only arena in my life where I'm still undefeated and going strong.

* * *

In Super Bowl XLIII, played in Tampa Bay on February 1, 2009, we faced a team I would soon come to love: the Arizona Cardinals.

With less than three minutes to play in the fourth quarter, the Cardinals' Kurt Warner hit Larry Fitzgerald for a 64-yard touchdown pass. We had been in control most of the game—we led 17–7 at halftime and 20–7 in the third quarter—but now we were suddenly down 23–20 with 2:30 left in the game.

On the sideline everyone looked to Ben. Man, he was a picture of steely, cocksure confidence. "We were built for this," he said. "We're built for this one moment. We got this." Before he ran out onto the field for our final drive, I huddled with Ben with the world watching. I looked him squarely in the eyes and I could see his immense self-confidence: There was no doubt in my mind that he was going to lead us to victory. I imagined that this was what it was like to look into the eyes of Joe Namath before he took the field in Super Bowl III. You can't win without your leader—your quarterback—exuding the confidence of a Douglas MacArthur, a Warren Buffett, a Caesar.

"It's now or never," Ben told the guys in the huddle. "Now or never!"

Starting at our 12-yard line because of a holding penalty, Ben lined up in the shotgun. We were running our two-minute drill offense but we only had one wide receiver and one tight end who were healthy. Nate Washington had a separated shoulder and Hines Ward had a bum knee. So our only legitimate threats on the field were wide receiver Santonio

Holmes and tight end Heath Miller. "Throw it to those two guys," I told Ben before he jogged onto the field.

Looking at the long field in front of us, I simply hoped to march into field goal range and try to put the game into overtime. But then Ben started doing his thing, pump-faking and shifting in the pocket and buying extra time. On first-and-20 he hit Santonio for 14 yards. On third-and-six he found Santonio again for 13 yards for a first down. A few plays later, with the clock ticking, Ben hit Santonio 10 yards down the field, and Santonio spun and sprinted to the Arizona six-yard line. Now 48 seconds remained in the fourth quarter.

To this point in the game we had used almost every play in our red-zone offense, and I absolutely hate running the same play twice in a game—I always believe that if defense sees a play once, it's near impossible to fool them twice.

On first down I called a play that I thought would win us the game. Ben pump-faked and then drilled a perfect pass to Santonio in the back of the end zone. Victory, I thought. But the ball slipped through Santonio's hands.

On the sideline I'm thinking, *Shit, now what am I going to call? That was our Super Bowl ring right there.* But then— and this happened in a matter of seconds—I remembered a play from earlier in the game that should have worked but was derailed because the Cardinals blitzed us and we didn't pick it up. The name of the play was "74 Scat Flasher Z Level." I quickly radioed it in to Ben.

In the shotgun, Ben took the snap. Our line did its job, holding the four Cardinal rushers at bay. This meant Ben had time to work through his progression. He first looked to running back Willie Parker, who was covered in the flat. Then he spotted Hines Ward in the end zone. Cardinal defenders surrounded Hines, but Ben pumped the ball his way anyway. That made a few of the Arizona defensive backs turn in Hines's direction. And that heartbeat of motion—a split-second move of the ball from where he would heave it—was all Ben needed.

He spotted Santonio sprinting toward the right corner of the end zone. There were three defenders in front of Santonio, but Ben unleashed his fastball anyway. He later told me the moment he let it rip he thought the ball was going to be intercepted.

But oh, what a pass it turned out to be. Ben placed it perfectly, high and outside, to a spot where only Santonio could snag it. Santonio threw his hands up and the ball hit his mitts perfectly. It was on our sideline and I was staring right at it. Santonio looked like a ballerina as he tapped his feet inbounds and fell out of the field of play.

After the game everyone talked about the catch—everyone, that is, but me. I couldn't believe the throw. To this day, I think that's a play that only one player in NFL history was capable of making, and that's Ben. He pump-fakes and delivers a fastball on the money as well as anyone in the game. That was unquestionably a Hall of Fame–worthy pass. Considering the magnitude of the moment, it should go down as one of the great throws in NFL history. We won the game 27–23 to capture our second Vince Lombardi Trophy in three years.

Up to that time in my career, that was as good as it got for me as a play caller: winning a Super Bowl with a two-minute drive. We had a hell of a party that night at the Intercontinental

Hotel in Tampa. My entire family was there, and we moved among three different ballrooms that each had a band playing.

Late that night—or, early that morning, I should say—I spotted Ben. We had all been given Super Bowl robes and he was wearing his over his street clothes. He had a cigar hanging from his mouth and a big, beautiful smile plastered on his face. Such moments of triumph always seem to pass by too quickly, so I really tried to slow time down that night, to savor each interaction with each player, to hug my wife and kids especially hard as we partied the night away.

But the feeling of winning a Super Bowl, for me at least, isn't as much joy as it is pure relief. The losing Super Bowl team is always quickly forgotten, and you are acutely aware of that in the days leading up to the big game. The pressure is enormous. So when that final whistle blew and we were crowned world champions, I finally felt like I could relax and take my first deep breath in months.

That feeling lasted for about three weeks. Even though I was actually booed during our victory parade in Pittsburgh—a fan yelled at me to "get a fullback," to which I replied, "Never!"— we celebrated like it was a once-in-a-lifetime New Year's Eve. But shortly after the parade the coaching staff had to start thinking about free agency, the NFL Combine, the draft, and the coming season. You can't pat yourself on the back for too long in the NFL because you can bet your ass other teams aren't. They're working. We knew that. So after three weeks, we quit talking about the victory. It was time to move on, and we did.

* * *

In 2010, Ben was suspended for the first four games of the season for violating the NFL conduct policy. In March of that year he had been investigated by police in Milledgeville, Georgia, for an alleged sexual assault that occurred in the women's restroom of the Capital City nightclub. Ben emphatically told me nothing happened. I'm not a police officer and I wasn't there; I'm Ben's coach and it's my job to prepare him to play football. No charges were ever filed against him, but the NFL suspended him for the first month of the 2010 season.

I wasn't allowed to speak directly to Ben during his suspension, but I knew he was working out with George Whitfield, a former college quarterback at Tiffin University in Ohio who specialized in training quarterbacks out of his own academy in San Diego. I had a relationship with George, so I would email him our practice scripts and our play script so Ben could keep his head in the game, even though he wasn't allowed inside the Steelers practice facility. I also told George the different fundamentals I wanted Ben to focus on while he was away from the team. Ben's early success actually stunted his growth, I thought, because he wasn't working as diligently as he needed to be. He thought he had it all figured out. But he didn't. I especially wanted Ben to shorten his stroke—his throwing motion—because he had a little too much wind-up and was taking too long to release the ball.

Ben had never been a drill guy. But that month away from the game changed him, as it should have. So many times in life we don't appreciate what we have until it is taken away from us, and I think during his suspension Ben fell in love with football all over again. He gained new respect for the game and a new respect for drill work. The gifted QBs oftentimes don't work on fundamentals, because everything comes so natural to them. Ben fell into this category. But his approach changed during the suspension. On several occasions George reported to me that Ben was working hard and that he believed he'd be ready to play once the suspension was over.

George was right: In Ben's first game back against the Cleveland Browns, he completed 16 of 27 passes for 258 yards, three touchdowns, and one interception in our 28–10 win. He looked like he was in midseason form. Ben would finish the 2010 regular season with a 9–3 record, 3,200 yards passing, 17 touchdowns, and a career-low five interceptions. We entered the playoffs as the AFC's number two seed.

On October 3 of that season I celebrated my fifty-eighth birthday. This was significant because it made me what I called "bulletproof." The NFL had instituted a rule a few years earlier that stated if your years of service in the league plus your age added up to seventy-five, then you could retire and they would "bridge" you until you turned sixty-five (meaning they would pay for your health care and you could access a special "bridge" retirement account) and were eligible for Social Security and Medicare. So now, even if I lost my job, my family would still be financially set.

The night I turned fifty-eight I called my old friend Carl Smith, a longtime NFL coach who was then the quarterback coach of the Seattle Seahawks. Smith's college nickname was Tater and he's three years older than me.

"Tater, we made it, baby," I said. "You know what? It's different now. I don't give a shit about what anybody thinks of my play calls. I don't have to please anybody. I'm going to do whatever the hell I want now from here on out because it doesn't matter."

Tater let out a good laugh. Thing was, I wasn't really kidding.

In the AFC Championship Game against the Jets, we held a 24–19 lead in the fourth quarter and we had the ball on their 40-yard line. The whistle for the two-minute warning had just blown and Ben was standing on the sideline next to me when I told him we were going for the win.

"Screw a running play," I said. "Kill shot time."

Ben completed a 14-yard pass to Antonio Brown to seal the victory. We were going to our second Super Bowl in three years.

There is nothing worse than when the confetti falls on your shoulders after the Super Bowl and it's not for you.

We had a chance to win the franchise's seventh title in the fourth quarter of Super Bowl XLV, on February 6, 2011. Trailing Green Bay by six points with 2:07 to play, we started a drive at our 13-yard line. After a five-yard reception by Hines Ward and two incomplete passes, Big Ben's fourth-down pass was intercepted. We lost 31–25.

In the offseason I was a little surprised I didn't get any invitations to interview for a head coaching position. I know I'm not a head coach out of central casting—hey, I've never met a four-letter word I didn't like—but man, I had just helped the Steelers reach two Super Bowls in three years with our offense. At this point I figured I'd probably never become a head coach, and I was fine with that. I was perfectly happy in Pittsburgh.

Ben and I continued to have success with each other through the 2011 season, when Ben threw for over 4,000 yards. After losing to Denver and Tim Tebow in the first round of the playoffs in January 2012, I met with Mike Tomlin, our head coach. Tomlin told me he was going to try to get me a raise in the offseason.

But a few days later, I was in the basement of our Reynolds Plantation home when Mike called. His voice sounded funny. I immediately knew something wasn't right.

"What's up?" I asked.

"I couldn't get you the raise," Mike said. "I couldn't get you the contract."

"That's all right," I said.

"No, no," Mike said. "I couldn't get you *any* contract."

"Are you firing me?" I asked.

"I would never do that," he said.

"Do I have a contract?" I asked.

"No," Mike said.

"Well, then you're firing me," I said.

Mike asked me to come to Pittsburgh so we could talk. I told him hell no and I told him not to fly to Georgia to see me. I was hot, man. I was pissed.

The biggest thing with me is loyalty. If you prove to me that you've got my back, then, brother, I'll always have yours. I may reassign an assistant coach if it's not working out, but I will never fire one. Never. If you're coaching for me you're family, and that's not how I treat my family.

I walked upstairs and told Chris that I had been fired from Pittsburgh. She broke down and cried. Chris wasn't crying because I had lost my job—shit, I had been fired almost too many times to count—but she was upset because she felt betrayed by Mike, who she had put up on a pedestal. I still hold Mr. Rooney on a pedestal. The Steelers owner, who passed away in April 2017, was one of the classiest men in all of football. May he rest in peace.

But I was bitter for a long time about being fired. But now I thank Pittsburgh for letting me go. Otherwise I wouldn't have gotten the chance to coach Andrew Luck or had the opportunity to become head coach of the Arizona Cardinals.

So thank you, Pittsburgh.

Thank you so, so much.

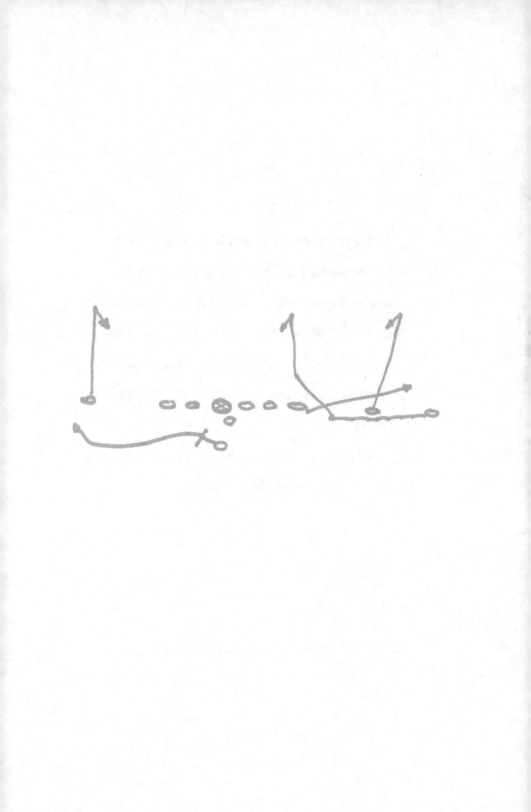

During practices B.A. is as intense as any coach I've ever been around. He can yell at you with such colorful language that it's almost like he gives you new words that you need to look up. But then after practice he'll ask you about your mom, your sister, your girlfriend—basically, anything that doesn't have to do with football. He truly cares, and that's why players across the NFL love the guy.

— ANDREW LUCK

CHAPTER 7

ANDREW LUCK

I was ready for the good life—golf and long, lazy afternoons hanging out at the lake. In January 2013, I was okay with the prospect that my coaching career was over. More important, my wife was absolutely overjoyed.

After Mike Tomlin fired me as the offensive coordinator with the Steelers—the grapevine said that Pittsburgh's ownership didn't like my aggressive style and wanted a more running-based offensive attack—I believed that my headset-wearing days were over. And I was fine with that. I had always wanted to be a head coach in the NFL, but I refused to pander to anyone. I never hired an agent. Shit, I never even put together a résumé. I always figured if you needed to know my background, you could just look it up in any number of team media guides.

We were financially set and now it was important to me to spend more time with my family. But I still wanted to keep my hands in the game, even if I wasn't a full-time, paid coach. So I took a job preparing guys for the NFL draft. My first client was Oklahoma State wide receiver Justin Blackmon. Brother, I thought I had it made. This was going to be a real sweet gig: I wouldn't have to travel very much, which meant more sunset drinks with Chris on the porch; I'd still be interacting with young players; and now I'd have extra pocket money for golf.

I'd only been out of work about a week when I flew to Stillwater, Oklahoma, to meet with Justin. He was battling some issues with alcohol—at the time he had one DUI on his record—but I thought he was a really good kid and a phenomenal athlete. I put him through drills to prepare him for the upcoming NFL Combine, and he just blew me away. At 6'1", 210 pounds, he had rare abilities. He could run a 4.4, jump through the roof, and had terrific hands. On talent alone, he was a top-three pick.

I also put him through mock press conferences and interviews to replicate the intense scrutiny he'd encounter at the Combine. He did a fine job, I thought. We then had a long talk about his drinking, and he assured me that it wouldn't be an issue moving forward. I believed him—and so did the coaching staff of the Jacksonville Jaguars, who would select Justin with the fourth overall pick in the draft. Sadly, however, this story didn't have a happy ending: Justin never could shake his alcohol demon. The NFL suspended him twice for violating the league's substance abuse policy and he was charged with two more DUIs. He hasn't played a down in the NFL since 2013.

But after working with Justin in Stillwater over the course of a weekend, I believed I had found what I would do in the next phase of my life. I figured I'd sign up a few potential top picks each year, prepare them for the draft, and then spend about nine months each year with Chris and my golf sticks.

I flew from Stillwater back to Georgia. I spent a few days at the lake and then Chris and I began the drive to Pittsburgh, where we planned to pack up our apartment. By this point we had become experts in the art of moving—a side benefit to being fired nine times—and now we thought we were making the final move of our career. We were going to our "Forever Home," as Chris calls it, in Reynolds Plantation, Georgia.

Driving north on I-75 to return to the Steel City one last time, Chris and I talked about what was next for us. Listen, I don't look backward. It's not my style. There's nothing to see in the rearview mirror. Life is to be lived, not reviewed. You learn from your past and then you move on, simple as that.

And I had moved on. But then, just after we rolled over the Pennsylvania state line in our black GMC Denali, my cell phone buzzed. I was driving so I handed my phone to Chris. She answered. On the other end of the line was Chuck Pagano, who a few hours earlier had just been named the head coach of the Indianapolis Colts.

Chuck said hello to Chris—we knew the Pagano family well—and then she handed the phone to me. But before I could say anything, Chris turned to me, narrowed those beautiful blue eyes of hers, and said, "You're going to take this damn job, aren't you?"

I grinned at my lovely wife. I then told Chuck how happy I was that he'd landed the Colts job.

"What's this retirement bullshit?" Chuck said. "I need you with me."

"Well, what are you talking about?" I asked.

"We're going to have a young quarterback," Chuck replied. "I need you to guide him and run our offense."

"I'll be on a plane to Indy tomorrow," I said.

We spoke a few more minutes. After I hung up, I looked over at Chris.

"What the hell," she said, shaking her head. "Life can really be a bitch. A real bitch."

That was her way of conveying a simple message: The lake would wait; we were heading to Indy, another future.

I only had one hesitation about taking the job as the offensive coordinator of the Colts: The franchise was releasing Peyton Manning.

A few days before Chuck Pagano called me in January 2014 and offered me the chance to run his offense, I had talked to Peyton on the phone. He asked me to come to Indianapolis to check out his arm. Peyton had been through four different surgeries on his neck, and now he believed he was regaining his arm strength. He wanted me to watch him throw and give him an honest assessment of his arm.

Then I got the job. After I met with Chuck and signed my contract, I never even saw Peyton. After Peyton was told by owner Jim Irsay and Chuck that he was being let go, he held a press conference. As always, he was class personified. He said goodbye to Colts fans in an emotional press conference. His speech of that day should be required viewing for high school

football players across the country, because he lyrically artic-
ulated how much we all should respect the game. I wanted to
be there, but I couldn't bring myself to attend Peyton's public
farewell. It just hurt too damn much.

There is a principal tenet about my relationship with my
quarterbacks—they are my family, even when I'm not their
coach. When my quarterback hurts, I hurt. That's just how
tight my bond is with them. I knew Peyton was torn up about
leaving Indianapolis, and that upset me to the nth degree.

But I agreed with the decision by Jim Irsay to move on
from Peyton. Jim is a very smart man. And he knew he had a
rare opportunity in front of him: The Colts had the number
one overall pick in the upcoming draft, and there were two
quarterbacks who we thought could be worthy of that selection: Andrew Luck out of Stanford and Robert Griffin III out
of Baylor. My first big job at Indy this time around was identi-
cal to the first time around—I was to recommend which of the
two who we should take.

I went out to Stanford to meet with Andrew. He was so
smart. And he's got a goofiness that is so honest it's uncannily
cool. But it's his intelligence that leaps out at you like a bur-
glar from the bushes; I don't know if I ever talked to a player
who is that smart. I remember telling him to draw up a play on
the board, erase it, walk out of the room, then come back and
teach me that exact play. We did this several times and in a few
instances when he came back in I'd say something incorrect
about a play to see if I could throw him off. But Andrew busted
me every time and told me he knew the game I was playing
with him. What's more, when he repeated the plays to me, he

used the exact words—and I mean verbatim—that I had used. Andrew's brain—his memory—was incredibly impressive.

I got together with RG3 at the Combine in Indianapolis. He was sharp. He could tell you everything about the spread offense that he had run at Baylor. But I was concerned about him making the switch from the spread to the pro-style attack that we used. That was a big factor for me. I thought Andrew was more NFL-ready.

At 6'4", 235 pounds, Andrew was also bigger than RG3, who stood 6'2" and weighed 220. I believed Andrew was better suited to absorb the pounding an NFL quarterback endures during the season. They both were talented guys, no question, but I ended up supporting Andrew as our pick because he was spectacularly smart and he simply seemed to be a now-ready NFL quarterback in every respect, a guy who would be the leader of our franchise on day one. And without Peyton, it was something that we needed, badly.

I also loved the fact that Andrew came from a football family—and a worldly background, which I discovered during my research in preparation for the draft. I learned that Oliver and Kathy Luck, along with one-year-old Andrew, had moved to Germany in December 1990. Three more children—Mary Ellen, Emily, and Addison—would be born in Europe.

Oliver, a former quarterback at West Virginia who set school records for touchdowns and completions, had been named the general manager of the Frankfurt Galaxy of the fledgling Europe-based World League of American Football. He eventually became the president of the league, which was renamed NFL Europe in 1998 and served as a developmental league for the NFL.

Oliver has a quick, impressive mind; he spurned offers from Harvard and Yale to attend West Virginia, where he won the Louis D. Meisel Award, given to the student-athlete with the highest grade point average as a senior. He hoped Europe, where his family would live for a decade, would be a giant classroom for Andrew.

In the days before the draft, I found out that Oliver rarely talked football with his oldest child, who was more interested in playing soccer and basketball with his European buddies. But then Andrew found a VHS tape of a 1985 Houston Oilers–San Diego Chargers game. There on the grainy video, eight-year-old Andrew saw his dad, then the starter for the Oilers, complete 24 of 42 passes for 286 yards and one touchdown in Houston's 37–35 win. Oliver Luck had outplayed future Hall of Fame quarterback Dan Fouts.

"Andrew must have watched that one game a thousand times," Oliver said.

Some Sundays, father and son stayed up deep into the night to watch NFL games that aired over the U.S. military's Armed Forces Network. Oliver showed Andrew things—such as how Dan Marino held the ball next to his ear so he could release it quickly—but he mostly just answered Andrew's questions, never wanting his son to feel forced to follow his footsteps into the game.

But slowly, Andrew became increasingly intrigued by the sport. He and his dad sat together into the small hours of a Monday morning in January 1998 watching Super Bowl XXXII; Andrew was mesmerized by John Elway "doing the whirlybird"—his description of Elway's memorable dive for a first down against the Green Bay Packers.

Oliver took Andrew to several NFL Europe games, where Andrew saw Amsterdam Admirals quarterback Kurt Warner and his pinpoint passing lead the league in yards and touchdowns in 1998. The feathery touch Warner displayed in stadiums from Barcelona to London became one of Andrew's most vivid images of the league. Another sweet memory for Andrew was playing games of catch with his dad in their yard in Frankfurt. It was perhaps the most red-white-and-blue experience of his early childhood.

Eventually, Andrew pressed his father about his own NFL career, and Oliver told him about life as a Houston Oiler, where he backed up a veteran named Archie Manning in 1982 and '83.

The low man on the quarterback totem pole in Houston, Oliver was conscripted into a most unusual duty: babysitting. Manning, who commuted on Southwest Airlines three or four times a week to Houston from his home in New Orleans, would land at the airport and be greeted by Oliver. Archie would then hand off his two oldest boys to his personal gofer of a backup.

Archie would head to the Oilers football facility, while Oliver chaperoned Cooper Manning and his younger brother Peyton around town, stuffing them into his Mazda RX7 and taking them to get ice cream, grab a hamburger, or play miniature golf. The car was only a two-seater, so it was usually six-year-old Peyton who had to crouch in the hatchback.

Oliver, of course, never could have fathomed he was toting around the child who would one day become the Colts' starting quarterback—and the man whose own unborn son would replace him as the starter in 2012.

"That was the beginning of a long-standing relationship between the Lucks and the Mannings," Oliver said. "It's gotten interesting over the years, but we've always had a wonderful friendship."

Recognizing he was never going to be a top-flight NFL starter, Oliver took law school classes at night and during the offseason at the University of Texas while playing for the Oilers. He earned his law degree, cum laude, in '87. His wife, Kathy, who already held a master's degree in social work, also picked up her juris doctor from the University of Texas. Clearly, the Luck children come from an impressive gene pool.

Oliver played for Houston from 1982 to 1986. He walked away from the NFL after five seasons—just long enough to qualify for his NFL pension—because there were so many other fruits in life to taste. That was a lesson he emphasized time and again to Andrew.

As a child, Andrew loved architecture. Historic buildings held his eyes like nothing else in Europe, and he was always asking his father how things were built. In his childhood room in Frankfurt, he was the Gustave Eiffel of Lego construction.

Andrew flourished on the soccer field and the basketball court. Those sports honed his hand-eye-foot coordination, his ability to discern passing angles, and his peripheral vision. As he matured and the seasons on the pitch and the court passed—for the record, he usually communicated with his teammates in German—he began to view both sports like chess matches; the movements of each player needed to be choreographed with the others because the team would flounder if one player made a misstep.

He developed, as basketball great Bill Bradley once described, a sense of where you are. "Those sports help you understand how people relate to each other in space," said Andrew.

"Those were the two best sports Andrew could play to get him ready to be a quarterback because they emphasize team movement and passing angles," said Oliver. "Overall, I think the impact of living in Europe—where Andrew was exposed to different languages, different cultures—is that it made him a little more inquisitive about the world. He realized that the world was big and you should ask questions, be open-minded and tolerant."

When the Lucks returned to the United States in 2001— Oliver was named the CEO of the Houston Sports Authority, which builds stadiums—one of Andrew's first questions wasn't whether he could try a juicy longhorn steak or play football in Texas. Rather, he asked his father, "Why aren't there any trains in the United States?"

At age eleven, Andrew was already asking the most important question a quarterback can: Why?

Andrew is a voracious reader of books. It is as if written words speak secrets to him. No subject is off-limits: religion, politics, biography, history. During his rookie season he revealed to a teammate that he was reading a narrative on the wild and riveting history of . . . concrete. Imagine that!

Did you guys know the Roman Colosseum was built mostly of concrete? And the Hoover Dam as well? That is a young man committed to unraveling as many yarns of life's complexities as possible.

Shortly after returning to the United States, Andrew began doing what virtually all twelve-year-old boys do in the Lone Star State: He played Pop Warner football. For two seasons, Oliver was his coach. The boy wanted to play quarterback, mostly because that was the position he saw his old man master on that VHS tape.

Andrew was a natural, as if everything his father knew about the game had been transferred to him via genetic code. Talking about why his son is successful at football, Oliver cited the book *Freakonomics*, in which authors Stephen J. Dubner and Steven D. Levitt argue the number one trait that determines whether a child will become a professional baseball player is not size, speed, or education; it is simply if his father was a professional baseball player. It's hard to argue with that logic.

At Stratford High in Houston—where Andrew was usually in one of two places: the library or the football field—he threw for 7,139 yards and 53 touchdowns. He was, according to Rivals.com, the nation's fourth-ranked pro-style quarterback in 2008. He had an uncanny touch on his throws, like Kurt Warner lighting up the old stadiums in Europe.

The one knock on Luck was that he didn't have elite arm strength, but what recruiting analysts didn't know—because Andrew didn't tell them—was that he rarely unleashed his fastball because he was afraid it would be too hard for his receivers to catch.

Andrew was the co-valedictorian of his class, and he dreamed of designing stadiums. The venues he saw in his youth throughout Europe—iconic structures such as Wembley Stadium in London and Rheinstadion in Düsseldorf—remained vivid in his mind. "I was infatuated with stadiums," he said.

Nick Saban, Bob Stoops, and virtually every big-name coach in the nation traveled to Stratford High to recruit Andrew, but he wanted to attend a school that had as much heritage in academics as athletics. By his junior year, he had narrowed his list of schools to five: Stanford, Purdue, Northwestern, Virginia, and Rice.

Stanford's coach at the time, former NFL quarterback Jim Harbaugh, was smitten with Andrew the first time he met him. Aside from Andrew's prototypical size and 4.6 forty-yard speed, Harbaugh was most impressed by the testimonials of Luck's teammates, each of whom expressed unequivocal admiration for their quarterback.

"Andrew is just so sharp mentally, so quick-minded," said Harbaugh back in January 2011. "And then just the easy personality to be around. He's like a dolphin; you know, he's really smart, he's always having fun and he's laughing and joking. . . . He's just so technically sound, so good with his mechanics, so great with his eye discipline."

Andrew majored in architectural design at Stanford. In the summer of 2009, he was a corporate sales intern with the San Jose Earthquakes of Major League Soccer. The following spring, for one class, he helped design a disaster-relief shelter and community for a site outside of Port-au-Prince, Haiti, after a 7.0-magnitude earthquake shattered the country.

From afar, several of us in the NFL wondered: Is Andrew Luck too good to be true?

* * *

It was important to Andrew to earn his degree, so after consulting with a longtime family friend—Peyton Manning, who had stayed in school for his senior year at Tennessee—he returned to "the Farm" for his senior year. In 2011, Andrew's final year at Stanford, the football coaches were so confident of their starting quarterback that they freighted him with more responsibility than most NFL QBs carry. Luck went to the line of scrimmage with three plays, and, depending on the defensive alignment he saw, he'd choose which play to run. That year, he led the Cardinals to an 11–2 record, good for seventh in the final Associated Press ranking.

I can still vividly remember the first time I knew we had won a once-in-a-decade jackpot by selecting Luck with the number one overall pick of the 2012 draft. At Andrew's first mini-camp that June, he walked into his first huddle. He then called his first play using terminology no one else had yet learned.

By day one of practice, Andrew had memorized the playbook. After the very first play all the linemen looked at each other dumbfounded, asking, "Who is this guy? What's he talking about?" But Andrew had the play and the terminology correct. It was just that none of the other players knew it yet.

He then started calling audibles and protection schemes that none of the other offensive players had heard of—and yet they were all 100 percent right out of our playbook. When the coaches told the other players that Andrew's calls were correct, the players just smiled at each other and nodded their heads. That was when they knew it: Their quarterback—our QB—of the future had arrived.

Andrew excelled at play action, and he was as gifted as any rookie I'd ever been around throwing intermediate-length anticipatory passes. One reason for his success was that no matter what happened immediately in front of him, he always kept his eyes downfield—just like all the greats who have played the position. Even when he felt the pressure of oncoming linemen and was forced out of the pocket, he always had his eyes trained on his receivers. With Andrew, a play was never really over—another trait of the truly talented NFL quarterback.

Andrew also won over the locker room in record speed. How? I remember seeing him talking nonstop with Josh Chapman, a nose tackle out of Alabama who we selected with the 136th overall pick of that 2012 draft. When the two met for the first time, Andrew peppered his draft mate with questions that had nothing to do with football: *What's it like to live in Alabama? Is it fun playing in the SEC? What's Nick Saban like? What do you like to do for fun?*

And just like that, the two became fast friends.

Neither Andrew's mind nor his wonderment ever quit working. I remember one of the first times he walked into Lucas Oil Stadium. He gazed up into the rafters, his eyes shining in awe, as if beholding the great Roman Colosseum for the first time. "This is so well done," he said to no one in particular. "The industrial look is just perfect. Just perfect."

On the second day during Andrew's first mini-camp with us, I wore black shoes, black socks, and a black undershirt out to practice. I purposely walked by the defensive backs, who were out on the field stretching. Jerraud Powers and Antoine Bethea looked up and down at me and started laughing.

"Where are you going?" they asked.

"A funeral," I replied.

"Whose?" Jerrod asked.

"Y'all's," I said, "because Andrew killed you yesterday." The two laughed again, but they knew and I knew that, after only one practice, it was clear Andrew was going to be a top-notch player in the NFL.

There were times during that first mini-camp that I'd stand off to the side and simply watch Andrew throw passes on "the driving range," as we called our separate practice field for quarterbacks and receivers. I was hypnotized by what I saw. Andrew would make every throw imaginable from every conceivable arm angle at every range of speed. He had, and used, every club in the bag, so to speak.

After practice Andrew would come into my office and ask a shitload of the most wide-ranging and most relevant questions about football. He wanted to know what type of play we would call in a range of specific down-and-distance situations and what he should look for in the defenses against our various plays. And once you answered his questions, you just knew he got it; he wouldn't need to re-ask the question or worry about the situation any longer. When he knew something, he really knew it. Then once our football business was over, we'd talk about our families. I loved to kid him about growing up in Europe, being a soccer junkie and an architecture nerd. He was the most well-rounded quarterback I'd ever coached.

That doesn't mean I wasn't hard on Andrew on occasion, especially when he needed a talking-to. During his first training camp in 2012, he came off the practice field one afternoon after misreading a defensive coverage and throwing an interception in a scrimmage. "I fucked that up," he told me. "Man, did I screw that up."

"Why the hell did you do that?" I asked. "But listen, it's okay, dude. Let's move on. We're learning here. Remember that. Every play is a chance to learn."

There is a fine line in coaching between motivating a quarterback by yelling at him and having those verbal bombs napalm his confidence. Make no mistake, I can be a world-class screamer—heaven help the quarterback who falls asleep in a meeting or any player who takes my damn parking spot— but I'm always searching for ways to become both loved and feared at the same time.

It's a coaching philosophy I learned from the best coach I've ever come across: Paul "Bear" Bryant.

In January 1981, when I was twenty-eight years old, I drove my little Pontiac Astre into Tuscaloosa to talk to the Bear. I had spent the previous three years as an assistant at Mississippi State, where as the passing game coordinator I had been a part of our 6–3 upset of Alabama the previous fall.

Coach Bryant was looking for a running backs coach. My former coach at Virginia Tech, Jimmy Sharpe, had set up the interview—contacts and having people vouch for you in coaching, as in all professions, are essential. From Sharpe, I learned that Coach Bryant had been impressed with my work with Dave Marler, our kicker at Mississippi State who had thrown for 429 yards two years earlier against Alabama.

"Go visit with Coach for ten, fifteen minutes and see what happens," Sharpe told me.

And so I did. I walked into Coach Bryant's office and immediately took a seat on a little sofa, which I swear he had the legs cut off. When you sat on that sofa you had to look up at Bryant, which of course gave him a home-field advantage in his office.

Coach Bryant sat behind his massive oak desk, a string of smoke rising from a Pall Mall dangling from his lips, silently inspecting me for a few moments. Then the Bear said in his gravelly drawl, "I hear you have a way with young black players. Is that true?"

Coach Bryant knew that I had grown up with African Americans and that many of my best friends in the world were black. "Well, Coach," I said, "I don't know about that. I don't care what color the kids are. Hell, they can be green, red, white, or gold for all I care. But I do know that I'm going to cuss them out if they screw up."

"I don't allow cussing," Bryant said. "It's a dollar a swear word."

"Shit, looks like I won't be getting a paycheck," I said.

At that moment, I figured I had blown my chance at the job. But the Bear leaned back in his chair and smiled like your favorite grandfather. That smile—big and bright—could disarm anyone.

A few days later I was back in Starkville when the phone at our little ranch house rang. It was Mrs. Paul Bryant.

"Now, your name, Arians, is that German or Dutch or French?" she asked.

"It's German, ma'am," I said.

"Why, that is such a pretty name," she said. "Paul is going to talk to you in a second."

Coach Bryant then came on the phone. "The job is yours," Coach said. "Come on over on Monday morning and we'll get it all set up."

I thanked Coach Bryant profusely and then hung up our rotary phone. Every young coach needs a big break, and this was mine, a momentous career changer. I now was going to work for the greatest college football coach in history, and I believed that this would turn me into a made man in the coaching world—if I kept busting my ass and quit cussing!

Then I looked at Chris. "Did you take the job?" she asked.

"Damn right I did," I said.

"Well, how much are you going to make?" she asked.

"Uh, shit," I replied. "I forgot to ask. I'm sure he'll give me a raise from the eighteen grand I'm making now. I'm sure of it."

A few days later I was back in Coach Bryant's office. He shook my hand and told me I was going to earn $27,000 a year. I quickly called Chris and told her we'd hit the jackpot.

Chris and I went house hunting in Tuscaloosa. I had gotten a check for $3,000 a few months earlier for helping Mississippi State win the Peach Bowl. Now I planned to use that stash as the down payment.

We found a place that had a pool. The house was infested with mice, but man, we wanted that pool. I went to the bank and told the loan officer that I had $3,000 invested in a money market with a Mississippi State booster and I'd call to have it wired over to the bank. Well, the money wasn't there; the booster had used it to try to save his failing business. The dude was bankrupt, which meant I'd never see that cash again.

Now I was in a bind. I was supposed to close on the house at 4 p.m. and I didn't have the cash for the down payment. I called Bryant. "Coach, I need some advice," I said. I then explained the pickle I was in.

Coach Bryant started laughing.

"This shit ain't funny, Coach," I said.

"You've learned a lesson," he said. "Don't ever give money to a booster! They're supposed to make you money, not the other way around. But don't worry. I'm on the board of that bank. I'll fix it up. You go on down there. You close at four."

So we did. Two years later, when I became the head coach at Temple and we sold our house, I discovered that there was $3,000 extra in the equity of the house. I asked the bank officer where the money had come from.

"Coach paid that," he said.

"I thought he only got the note changed," I said. "He never said anything."

"Nope," he said, "Coach Bryant took care of it."

Just then I learned another lesson from the greatest there ever was: Head coaches must always look out for their assistants.

Beginning on my first day in T-Town, I watched Coach Bryant closely, as if he was more my kindly teacher than my grizzled boss. He knew everybody's name in the building—from the janitors to the cafeteria workers to the secretaries—and could tell you their backstories. If a coach's secretary was having a bad day, the Bear would detect it and stop at her desk to offer a few encouraging words. Her day would suddenly be brightened. It was magic the way he dealt with people. He could read faces and body language better than anyone.

He certainly could read me. After I had been on the job about two weeks, I got called into a meeting. The NCAA had just banned part-time coaches from recruiting, and one of Coach Bryant's longtime assistants told me that I was going to become a part-time guy and therefore I needed to stop recruiting. I immediately walked down the hall and stormed into the office of Mal Moore, who was then Coach Bryant's offensive coordinator and closest friend.

"Mal, I didn't sign up for this shit," I said. "Fuck this, I quit."

I walked out of the building and drove home. Man, I was an arrogant young hothead. Thank God my wife was running errands; she would have gone after me like a shark after chum. With no one to talk to, I called Jimmy Sharpe and told him what had happened. He then phoned Coach Bryant, who apparently was on the golf course. Thirty minutes later Sharpe called me back and told me Coach Bryant was on his way to the office and that I needed to go meet him.

Nothing, I quickly found out, pissed off Bear Bryant more than getting pulled off the golf course. "What the hell is going on?" he gruffly asked me in his office.

"Coach, I take great pride in being a full-time coach," I said. "Recruiting is a part of that. If this was the job you offered me two weeks ago, I'd still be at Mississippi State. I'm not a part-time coach."

Coach Bryant slowly rose from his chair and stared at me intently, square in the eyes, as I sat on that tiny low-legged sofa.

"I don't speak out of both sides of my mouth, boy," he said. "You get your ass in that car of yours and you start recruiting. You good?"

"Yes sir," I said. "I am good."

And that was the end of me quitting on Bear Bryant. But there are times in life when you absolutely have to stand up for yourself. There are principles worth fighting for. Challenging the Alabama establishment was a big moment in my career.

But it wasn't like I suddenly became Bear's Chosen One. After every game the entire staff would gather in the film room and review every single play. Then Coach Bryant would go around the room and ask each position coach how his players performed.

When he'd get to me, he'd ask, "How'd the running backs play?"

"Good," I'd say.

"Did you watch the film?" he'd ask.

"Yes sir," I'd say.

"Well, shit, son," the Bear would say, "you must not know how to grade film."

I'd sit there boiling mad, then I'd go into his office after the meeting. "Do you want number grades? Letter grades? What do you want?" I asked.

"You're doing fine," Coach Bryant replied.

But then the same thing happened the next week, then the next, and the next. Each time I'd follow him into his office and ask what he wanted from me, and he'd reply the same way each time: "You're doing fine."

By the fifth week of the season I'd finally had enough. I

went into his office again and stood my ground. "Obviously I'm not doing fine, Coach," I said. "I want to know how the hell you want these guys graded. Just fucking tell me."

"You're doing a hell of a good job, Bruce," he said calmly. "A hell of a good job."

It turned out that Bear was just testing me. He knew I was cocky as hell and, in his own way, he wanted to bring me to my knees, which he did. It was brilliant.

Coach Bryant normally watched practice from his famous tower overlooking the field. Our running backs stretched right under the tower, and if we heard that chain jingle it meant Coach was coming down to chew some ass.

One day I thought I was about to get ripped a new one. Before practice I was going over film with my players when I heard a knock on the door. It was Miss Linda, Coach Bryant's secretary, and she wanted to know if we were going to practice today. "Yes, we are," I said. Then I looked at my watch: Practice started in minutes.

Man, we ran like hell out of that meeting room. The players quickly got dressed and we hustled onto the practice field. We didn't get a chance to stretch; the horn blew to signal the start of practice as we bolted out of the locker room.

The kids knew we were in trouble. I was in trouble. And we proceeded to have the best practice of the season, because all of us were on edge. After practice was over, we stayed on the field doing drills. I remember running around with a blocking dummy and my players flipping me over their heads. Most of the coaches went inside, but some of the older coaches stayed around to witness this approaching ass chewing.

Then Bryant came down from his tower and rolled up to us in a golf cart. My players couldn't wait to see me get my tail whooped.

Coach came up to me. "Shit, y'all ought to be late more often," he said. "That was the best damn practice y'all had all year."

Then he drove off. Another lesson learned: A head coach who is a little bit feared is a good thing.

The Bear, who sometimes played his three top quarterbacks in a game, treated each one like family. Every Saturday morning he would take a slow walk with his top QBs outside the team hotel. As they strolled together, Coach Bryant would tell them how much he believed in them, how much he cared for them, and how proud he was of each one. Coach Bryant's stern, stark stare could make you cry for your momma, but he was also as compassionate as any coach I'd ever worked with.

Why did his players work so hard for him? Because they knew he loved them. That was another lesson I learned.

In December 1982, I was in Florida on a recruiting trip when I stopped by the office of Howard Tippett, then a coach with the Tampa Bay Buccaneers. Opening his door, I saw that Howard was speaking with Jimmy Gruden, the team's running backs coach and father of sons Jon and Jay.

"You guys want to go get a drink?" I asked.

"Sure," Howard said. "By the way, Jimmy, this is the guy they should hire at Temple."

Jimmy looked at me closely. He had friends on the search committee at Temple, which had just fired its head football coach. "You want to be the head coach at Temple?" Jimmy asked.

"Sure," I said, shocked as hell and not really understanding what was going on.

"You're one of Coach Bryant's boys, right?" Jimmy asked.

"Yes, I am," I replied.

"Well, you need to get a résumé to the Temple people right away," Jimmy said.

Of course, I didn't have a résumé—that wasn't my style—so I express mailed the search committee an Alabama game program along with a letter stating that I wanted to become the next head coach at Temple. A few days later I was on a plane to Philadelphia to interview for the job. But first I had some important business to finish. The Bear was about to coach in his final game, and there was no way on God's green earth we were going to let him go out with anything but a win.

Up until this point in my career I never feared losing—until the 1982 Liberty Bowl.

On December 15, 1982, a week earlier, Bryant walked into a press conference in Tuscaloosa that aired on radio and TV. What he said brought the state to a standstill. There were reports of huge crowds in grocery stores across Dixie as people strained to hear his words. People driving to work pulled over onto shoulders of roads. Kids getting ready for school didn't run for their bus; instead they waited to learn what the Bear was going to say.

"There comes a time in every profession when we need to hang it up, and that has come for me as head coach at the University of Alabama," Coach Bryant said. "I'm a tired old man, but I'll never get tired of football."

We knew the world would be watching his final game in Memphis against Illinois. In the days leading up to the game the assistants hardly even slept; we were too nervous. "We can't lose this game," I must have said a thousand times before kickoff. "We just can't. They won't let us back into the state if we don't win. We can't let down Coach."

Days before his final game, *Sports Illustrated* writer John Underwood phoned the sixty-nine-year-old Bryant to ask him why he was hanging up his famous houndstooth hat.

"Because four damn losses is too damn many," Coach Bryant said, noting how many games we had lost that season. "I'm up to my ass in alligators, John. These new young coaches just have too much energy for me. We need someone younger."

"So you really are tired?" Underwood asked.

"Naw," said Bryant. "To tell you the truth, I feel great. I got so many things I've been wantin' to do for so long, and now I'm gonna get to 'em."

"Like what?" Underwood said.

"I'm not sure just yet," Bryant replied.

An estimated audience of 50 million tuned in to the game—millions around the world watched via the Armed Forces Network—to see Coach Bryant patrol the sideline one last time. We beat Illinois 21–15. I can still picture the smile on Coach Bryant's face as he hugged each and every one of his players in the locker room. He was so happy—and all of us assistants were so damn relieved.

I took dozens of mental snapshots of the Bear that night in Memphis. I still cherish my time with Bryant, and the things he did for me and taught me.

I didn't think I had a shot at the Temple job; I viewed the situation as a way to practice for when I'd really have a chance to become a head coach. The first people I met were Temple alum and former football star Bill Bernardo and his wife; Bill was on the search committee. They picked me up at the Philadelphia airport. As soon as I slid into their car, Bill asked me, "What would you like to do?"

I hadn't been back in Pennsylvania—my home state—for a few years, and I was dying for some old-school Italian food. "Man, I haven't had a good Italian meal in a long, long time," I said.

We went to Cuz's restaurant in Philly and ate until we nearly threw up—mounds and mounds of pasta and great quantities of red wine. We hit it off like long-lost friends. Bill told stories that put me on the edge of my seat, detailing how he was Bill Cosby's high school coach in Philadelphia. We had so much fun. By the end of the night I knew I had Bill and his wife on my side.

When I met with the vice president of the school, he asked me, "What's your philosophy?" I said I didn't have one. "But I do have a plan," I replied. "Our guys are going to go to class and they're going to graduate. We're going to win football games and we're going to be gentlemen and we're going to do something called the Fifth Quarter. Every Thursday night during the offseason I'll take one group of position players out into the community—to a hospital, an orphanage—and we'll give back. We'll show a highlight film and we'll just interact with the locals, which will help our kids grow and tighten our bond to the community."

Just like that, the VP was on board with me. Ten days later I was named Temple's next head coach. I was thirty, making me then the youngest head coach in all of college football. I was nervous and wasn't entirely sure I was ready to become a head coach, but I knew that I could always call Coach Bryant and ask his advice. I figured I might call him as often as once a week during the upcoming season.

I returned to Alabama to say my goodbyes. I walked into Coach Bryant's office and we embraced. I asked him questions about recruiting and organization, and then he told me about the nature of coaching—and life, really. "You get a job," he said, "and you do a hell of a job at it. You look for a better job until there ain't no better job. Then you work your ass to keep that job."

Then, before I left his office, Coach Bryant told me to carry one piece of wisdom with me for the rest of my days.

"Coach them hard," Coach Bryant told me, "and hug them harder later."

Those were the last words Bryant ever uttered to me. They became my guiding philosophy.

From that day forward I would try to find out what makes a player tick and continually build on the players' strengths and not prey on their weaknesses—just like Coach Bryant did. You always need to fix some of their weaknesses, but you first pad their confidence so that it grows, and then they can attack their weaknesses.

Like Coach Bryant, I would be hard on my players when we were on the field. But that's just coaching. The players need to know that I'm probably going to talk to them real ugly out on the field, but that has nothing to do with them personally or with their personality. Their football can suck and they can still be good kids. Don't take it personally. It's coaching, not criticism. Don't worry if I call you a "motherfucker" on the field. It's business, not personal.

And I vowed that day after leaving Coach Bryant's office that when I walked off the field with my players, I would hug the ones I had MF'd only moments earlier—just like Bryant did. I'd tell them we're going to get our football perfect, we're not going to beat ourselves, and now that we're done with football for the day we can talk all night long about our personal lives. And I would care about all my players, from the starting quarterback down to the third-string tight end. That's the prime role of a college head coach. He must help his players grow into young men of substance—men with confidence, character, and knowledge beyond the field. That's what makes coaching football so special.

Twenty-seven days after his last game, Bear experienced severe chest pains and was driven to Druid City Regional Medical Center in Tuscaloosa. By the next morning, though, he was feeling better and his family expected him to be released. Around noon he was sitting upright in his hospital bed with a yellow notepad in his hands, writing down reminders of things he wanted to do, words he wanted to say to those who mattered most to him. Ray Perkins, his replacement, stopped by to check in with his mentor; Bryant upbraided him for not being out on the recruiting trail.

Then, while in his bed eating lunch, Coach Bryant suffered a massive heart attack at 12:24 p.m. central standard time on January 26, 1982. Doctors frantically tried to revive him, but at 1:30, the call was made: The Bear was dead. In past years Coach Bryant had often ominously joked that he would "croak within a week" if he ever stopped coaching; it actually took twenty-eight days.

The news traveled quickly across Alabama, as if carried by the winter breeze that blew on that gray southern day. Grown men openly wept, like they'd just lost their most cherished family member. Farmers, steelworkers, lawyers, and stay-at-home moms stopped what they were doing, as if the realization that Bryant was gone took away the collective breath of the entire state in one seismic gut punch. Coach Bryant's passing was a lead story on all the national networks. "The Bear is dead," said Tom Brokaw on NBC. Local broadcasters labored to summon the strength not to break down on camera; some were more successful than others. Schoolteachers all across the state, many teary-eyed, stopped their classes to break the news to their students. That night President Ronald Reagan called Mary Harmon, Coach Bryant's widow, to offer condolences, to tell her that the nation was now mourning with her.

Bryant was the only coach in America, it was often said in the Heart of Dixie, who "can take his'n and beat your'n, and take your'n and beat his'n." When the Bear did suffer a rare loss, he'd appear on his weekly television show and the cohost would tell him, "The Lord just wasn't with us, Coach." Coach Bryant, without missing a beat, would respond with a growl, "The Lord expects you to block and tackle."

I was in my new office at Temple when I heard the news. I had worried about his health, but of course I never saw his end coming. He loved golfing and he had enough things on his mind to keep him busy, and I thought he'd live for years.

Two days after his passing, I flew to Alabama on a little twin-propeller plane and attended Bryant's funeral at the First United Methodist Church in Tuscaloosa. The tiny church couldn't accommodate the surge of well-wishers who had flown in from around the country to say goodbye to the Bear. Every head coach from the SEC was present, as were Nebraska's Bob Devaney and former Ohio State coach Woody Hayes. Hundreds of former players attended, as did reporters from as far as New York and Chicago. To enable everyone to see the short service, closed-circuit television cameras were installed and then relayed to monitors in two other nearby churches. After the final prayer was uttered at First United Methodist, eight Alabama players carried Bryant's casket down the steps of the church. As his body was placed in a white hearse, more than 200 photographers frantically clicked away, their flashes popping like lightning through the gray afternoon.

The funeral procession stretched three miles and consisted of nearly 300 cars, including six buses filled with former and present-day players and coaches. As the procession rolled down 10th Street in Tuscaloosa, thousands of locals stood four, five, and six deep to see Bryant a final time, waving at the hearse in respectful silence. The procession slowed when it passed Bryant-Denny Stadium, as if to give the coach one last look at the soaring cathedral where he made so many dreams come true, the place where his legend was forged. And then it pulled onto Interstate 20/59 and headed east for Birmingham.

On the interstate, cars and trucks and eighteen-wheelers pulled to the side. The drivers and passengers stood next to their vehicles in silence as Coach Bryant rolled toward his final resting spot. Overpasses were clogged with onlookers—men placed their fedoras over their chests, women wept, children in Crimson Tide jackets gazed in wide-eyed wonder at the spectacle. All along the fifty-five miles from Tuscaloosa to Elmwood Cemetery in Birmingham the interstate was lined with people young and old, Yankees and southerners, all compelled to stand in the chill of the winter afternoon and cry and grieve and tell stories about Paul William Bryant. To Alabamians, this was a state funeral, every bit as significant as a president being laid to rest in Arlington National Cemetery. The *Birmingham News* estimated that 250,000 people had witnessed the procession, which meant that one of every twelve residents of Alabama had bid farewell to Bryant in person.

I'd never seen such love for a head coach—and I never will again.

"It was a great blessing for Bruce to coach under Bear Bryant," Chris says. "Bruce became one of his many disciples, which meant he became respected all around the country. It changed how people in coaching viewed Bruce. Bear tested Bruce, and he wanted Bruce to stand up for what he thought was right and what he believed in. But Coach Bryant also valued everybody and he made you feel valued when you were with him. Bruce learned that from him and followed his example. That became part of who Bruce is. Bruce took his death hard—we all did—because he admired the Bear as much as his father. But Bruce didn't have time to be sad. He was a young coach and also a young father of two. He had to move on, and I know that's what the Bear would have told him to do. But it was definitely the end of an era for us."

When I was in my first year at Temple, trying to build the program and raise expectations, I constantly found myself uttering phrases that came straight from Coach Bryant's mouth. I also leaned on him for a few pregame one-liners.

Before we faced Boston College and their record-setting quarterback Doug Flutie in 1983, I told my players to gather around me in the locker room. The season before, Flutie had beaten us with a touchdown pass late in the fourth quarter, and now I didn't want any of our players to be nervous. So I used one of my favorite Bear Bryant sayings.

"Okay guys," I said, "I just want to see you bouncing across that field like you're running on an acre of titties."

The players doubled over in laughter, which was precisely why I said it. They went onto the field and had a blast, playing loose and fast. We lost 18–15. After the game one of my players approached me in the locker room.

"Coach," he said, "I'll never forget running across the field on an acre of titties."

Chris's life may have been more daunting than mine at Temple. We've always been a team—Chris could write her own book about the struggles of being a coach's wife—and in Philadelphia she really became the leader of our family. She had to sell our house in Tuscaloosa, find a new place in Philadelphia, and locate daycare for our two small children. She also enrolled in law school.

"It was tough being one of the few women in the class who was older and had a family to take care of," Chris says. "It was overwhelming. But the cool thing was that Bruce was able to bring in guys he'd coached with and played with. This is the thing about Bruce: He's incredibly loyal. So the staff became one big family at Temple.

"But by the sixth year, things weren't going the way we'd hoped. We knew we should have been winning bowl games. And Bruce was physically burned out. He was getting migraine headaches. He felt so responsible for his assistants and he was worried to death about their families. He's too stubborn to quit. So honestly it was a relief when he got fired. And amazing thing is, once he left Temple he never really got the migraines again. Of course, we never thought in a million years it would take so long for him to get another shot at being a head coach."

In Indianapolis, Andrew Luck required more hugs than oral hits. I knew I couldn't be as hard on him as I had been with other quarterbacks, because Andrew—a bighearted people pleaser—was more sensitive. So, with this co-valedictorian of the class of 2008 at Stratford High in Houston and Stanford graduate, I assumed the role of the encouraging professor.

On Saturday nights before games during Andrew's rookie year, 2012, I reviewed the game plan in painstaking detail with him. I would ask him what plays were his favorites, and then he'd weave them into the script of the first thirty plays the team would run.

Andrew excelled at throwing the long ball, and so I always put six long bombs in our plan for each game. I constantly told Andrew to take a shot if the defense appeared vulnerable based on its pre-snap formation. "If it's third-and-three and you got T.Y. [Hilton] on a deep route, then throw the fucking ball to T.Y.," I'd tell Andrew. "I don't care that we only need three yards. Throw the ball to T.Y."

Andrew also was extremely accurate on the up-the-seam throws. Seam balls separate quarterbacks. A seam ball is when you have three receivers running deep routes, two on the outside and one on the inside. The seam is the throw to the inside receiver; you have to get it over the linebacker and in front of the safety. It's one of the more difficult throws to make. A lot of quarterbacks can't find that guy in the middle. But Andrew could, and did, nearly every time. He made those tosses look effortless.

Late in Andrew's rookie year we traveled to Detroit. With about six minutes to play in the fourth quarter, we were trailing 33–21 when Andrew threw an interception. It looked like the game was over. But when he reached the sideline, he was fuming and yelling at the top of his lungs, "Let's win this. Let's win this." He then jogged over to the defensive unit. "You stop them and we'll win this game," he screamed. "Stop them."

Andrew had a little bit of a wild-eyed look on his face, and the defense responded. They forced a Lions punt and then Andrew hit LaVon Brazill for a 42-yard touchdown pass with 2:39 left, cutting our deficit to 33–28.

Andrew again came to the sideline and encouraged the defense to get a stop. They did. Then on the last play of the game, Andrew found Donnie Avery on a drag route—a shallow pattern across the middle of the field—for a touchdown. We won 35–33, and there was no doubt that Andrew's attitude had as much to do with our victory as the beautiful throws he made in the fourth quarter.

Andrew bloomed into a Pro Bowl player as a rookie. In his first year in the league, he set an NFL rookie record by throwing for 4,374 yards. He had Peyton's cerebral and analytical mentality, Ben's athleticism, and Kelly Holcomb's grit.

He was, to my eye, as close to a perfect young quarterback as I had ever seen.

He was the kind of quarterback I wanted to grow old with—or so I thought.

You carried the torch and all you went and did
was win nine ball games. You did it with dignity
and you did it with class. You're everything that I
always knew you were, and more.

– CHUCK PAGANO

CHAPTER 8

THE YEAR FOOTBALL BEAT CANCER

Chuck Pagano and I had been friends for years. I worked with his brother Johnny on the Saints staff in 1996, and Chuck and I coached together on the Browns staff under Butch Davis from 2001 to '03. I was Cleveland's offensive coordinator and Chuck was the secondary coach, and in practice my guys would go against his guys. We're both extremely competitive, and we always brought out the best in each other on the practice field.

We also just plain hit it off. There are a lot of assholes in the world of coaching—backstabbing is common and a lot of guys have personal agendas that don't match up with the team's agenda—but Chuck isn't one of them. He's a good, decent, hardworking man who is also a hell of a coach. After he hired me in 2012 to be his offensive coordinator with the Colts, we talked or texted at least daily, even if we had the day off.

I'll never forget that it was a little before noon on Sunday, September 30, 2012, when my cell phone rang. I was at our lake house in Reynolds Plantation, and Chris and I were preparing to head back to Indianapolis. We were finishing up our bye week. Our record was 1–2 at the time I answered the phone call.

The voice was Chuck's. I knew he hadn't been feeling well—he complained about being more fatigued than usual—and that he was planning to see a doctor during the bye week. At first he sounded like everything was okay. In his normal, confident voice, he talked to me about a few football-related things. But then, as quickly as one flips a light switch, the tone of his voice dropped. He told me he had some bruises and that his wife, Tina, had made him go to the doctor. Then he softly said it:

"I have leukemia."

Those words hung in the air for who knows how long. I was in a state of shock. Then, breaking the silence, he added, "Mr. Irsay wants you to coach the team."

Coaching was the furthest thing from my mind at that moment. Good God, my only concern was for my good friend who had rescued me from an early retirement. I knew he was in for a fight.

Back in 2007 I had my own health scare. Just after we won the Super Bowl with the Steelers, Ken Whisenhunt, our offensive coordinator, was hired to be the head coach of the Arizona Cardinals. Kenny wanted me to be his offensive coordinator in Arizona, but then Mike Tomlin offered me Ken's old job and promoted me from wide receivers coach to OC. If I had gone with Kenny to Phoenix, I never would have had time to get a physical. But because I stayed in Pittsburgh and didn't have to turn my life upside down, I decided to visit my doctor. It had been a long time since I'd seen him—too long.

A routine exam revealed that I had an elevated prostate-specific antigen (PSA) count. The doctor told me that too much PSA meant that I could have a benign enlarged prostate, or possibly cancer. He told me he was pretty sure it wasn't cancer.

Then he did a biopsy. He was wrong. I had cancer.

I had to wait about two months before my operation. Man, that was a long and agonizing time, not knowing if the cancer was contained or if it had spread to my bones. To keep my mind busy, I reviewed every play in the Steelers playbook. The doctors thought the cancer was growing but that it was restricted to the prostate, so I underwent a radical prostatectomy.

I remember waking up from the surgery, looking around and seeing no one—no doctor, no nurses, no family. Then I heard rounds of laughter out in the hallway; it was Chris, Jake, and Kristi. Then they came into my room with the doctor. He immediately lifted my sprits, telling me they had removed all the cancer and that it hadn't progressed out of my prostate. Then he announced, "I've got six beers in the refrigerator. You can have one beer with each meal."

That made my day. "Thank you, Doc!" I blurted.

I did have to wear a catheter under my clothes during the draft that spring, but I didn't care; I was so mightily relieved to be cancer free. Once you're told you have cancer, life changes. You realize how important your family is. You want to hug your kids more, spend more time with your wife. You realize how lucky you are to play a game for a living. After my cancer scare, I began speaking to different groups and telling anyone who would listen how important it is for men over forty—

especially those who have kids—to get checked for prostate cancer. It might have taken my life had I followed Ken Whisenhunt to the Arizona desert and not gotten checked.

My entire experience with cancer flashed back at me when Chuck said he had leukemia. I immediately slipped into the role of concerned friend. I asked him about his treatment, his doctor, his plan to fight the disease moving forward. I wanted to know everything about his chemotherapy—what was the dosage, how many treatments were needed, whether he would have to stay in the hospital. After probably thirty minutes of my badgering Chuck, telling him he was one of the toughest SOBs I'd ever met, and that he'd win the battle, we hung up.

But deep down, I was terrified for him. On the flight back to Indianapolis I flipped on my iPad and hunted online for information about his leukemia. I learned about the treatments and the recovery rates and the doctors who would be caring for him. After reviewing all the facts, I believed that Chuck was in very capable hands and would overcome his illness.

The next morning the team gathered for our regular 8:30 a.m. meeting in the auditorium at our practice facility. Chuck is as punctual as anyone I've ever met, and the players knew that too. At 8:31 Chuck wasn't there; I could sense that the players knew something was wrong.

Jim Irsay stepped in front of the team and broke the news, telling everyone that Chuck was in the hospital and wouldn't be getting out anytime soon. Then our team doctor broke down the disease and explained Chuck's game plan. The players were shocked by all of it. Heck, I was *still* in shock. But now I had a job to do. I never once considered myself the head coach; I was just keeping the seat warm until my good buddy got back on his feet. And that's what I told our players: *Chuck will always be the head coach of this football team.*

When I spoke to Mr. Irsay I told him I'd take the job as interim head coach on one condition: that we turn the light on in Chuck's office and not turn it off until he came back. Mr. Irsay thought that was a great idea. We put a plastic covering over the light switch so no one could flip it off. I wanted the light to be a sign to the players that said, "You may be tired at practice, but your head coach is fighting for his life." And I never allowed anyone to call me the head coach. Yes, I expanded my leadership role a little bit—I now decided if we were going to go for it on fourth down on Sundays and I addressed the players on Saturday nights in our team meeting on the eve of a game—but other than that the head coach of this team was still Chuck Pagano. I told everyone to just focus on doing their job, because that's what I was doing. We weren't going to change anything about how the locker room was run or managed. Everything would operate as it had before; only now Chuck wasn't around.

At our first practice without Chuck, I told the players to gather around me. I never write down what I'm going to say in a speech to my players; I'm an off-the-cuff guy who speaks from the heart. I always try to be as truthful as possible—I've got a low threshold for bullshit—and I wanted the players to know that we now had our mission for the season: We were going to play for Chuck.

I reminded the players that after every huddle we always yell, "One-two-three," and follow that with a word or phrase of the day, like "win," "finish," or "work hard." Then I said, "Aren't all these things that we yell together really what Chuck is? Doesn't he win? Doesn't he finish? Doesn't he fucking work hard?"

I could see I had the players' full attention at this point. They leaned in, their eyes intense with anticipation.

"Let's create a new tradition, right here, right now," I shouted. "Whenever we break a huddle we yell, 'One-two-three *Chuck*!'"

The players roared. Instantly I knew our guys were going to fight like hell for their coach. And so would I.

Our first game without Chuck was at home on October 7 against the Green Bay Packers. We put all of his game gear out in the locker every Sunday—for home games and away—and we downloaded every practice to his iPad. Chuck had every reason to live. Our goal was win enough games so he could come back and coach again that season. If that meant going to the playoffs, we were going to the playoffs—even though we had the worst record in the NFL the previous season.

When Mr. Irsay spoke to the team on that Monday in the auditorium, one of the last things he said was, "Beat the Green Bay Packers and take the game ball over to Chuck in the hospital." After those words flew from his lips, I said under my breath, "Shit, this is some fucking pressure."

So this was the second time in my life that I was afraid to lose a football game. I never thought I'd be as nervous before a game as I was when I jogged onto the field for Bear Bryant's final game of coaching, but now that same queasy feeling of more than three decades earlier gripped me to the core as I walked around the field at Lucas Oil Stadium before kickoff.

I spotted my son, Jake. We hugged, and then, grasping each other tight, we both started to cry. I'm not a crier— I hadn't shed a tear since my father's funeral—but now I was just overcome with emotion. My thoughts were wrapped around Chuck and the horror of cancer. Life just didn't seem fair at this moment, and yet it was also a defining moment of my career. I was now an acting head coach in the NFL, my lifelong dream had been achieved, but I wished to God it had never happened like this. The emotions arose, rattled my heart, and leaked from my eyes.

Jake was living in Birmingham. He had driven seven hours on that Monday to spend the week with me in Indy. He is my confidant, and on that first full day without Chuck I floated an idea to Jake: I told him I wanted to go no-huddle against the Packers.

Jake—an unfiltered soul like his old man—looked at me like I was the guy at the end of the bar who had stayed one drink too long. "Are you crazy?" he asked. "You can't do that in the first week on the job."

"But Andrew is ready," I said. "No risk it, no biscuit, baby."

I've always believed that the quarterback needs to run the show, not the offensive coordinator or head coach. When I'd had special quarterbacks in the past—most notably Peyton in Indy and Ben in Pittsburgh—we'd enjoyed great success operating out of the no-huddle offense. To make this work, though, the quarterback needs to understand the offense as thoroughly as the coaching staff does. Peyton did. Ben did. And I now believed Andrew would too.

But Andrew would only be starting the fourth game of his NFL career—it took Peyton and Ben years to be comfortable enough to run no-huddle—and so I knew he was going to make mistakes. But that was okay. One of Andrew's greatest strengths is that he's very good at forgetting bad plays. He learns from them and then erases them from his memory. It's uncanny. Some guys have their entire careers ruined because they can't move on from their mistakes. But not Andrew. He's a great forgetter.

During the week I told Andrew just to let it rip during the game. I encouraged him to take chances because I felt we needed to make big plays to have a chance at pulling off the upset against the Packers. And when I told him we were going to play fast and go no-huddle, his eyes lit up like the neon signs in Times Square—the exact response I wanted.

But the game couldn't have started out much worse for us. We missed a couple of throws on third down and fell behind 21–3 at halftime. Our guys were trying *too* hard. We all wanted so badly to give that game ball to Chuck, and I thought we played like we were scared to lose.

In the locker room at halftime I sensed how emotional the players were. It's possible for players to be *too* emotional—snot bubbles and tears don't win games—but our guys were in a good state. They were just trying too hard.

Plus, players perform their best when their emotions are on the edge. I knew this wasn't a time for me to give a rah-rah speech. I needed to be the sober-minded one in the room.

"Look, it's 21–3," I said. "We all can read the scoreboard. Now we just need to do our jobs and make some good things happen. Defense, you're up first. Get us a turnover. We can build momentum and win this thing. There's a lot of football still to be played." Then I ceded the speaking stage to Reggie Wayne and Cory Redding—I always like my veteran leaders to say a word a halftime—and they really got the guys' juices flowing.

Early in the third quarter our defense did exactly what I had asked. Jerraud Powers intercepted an Aaron Rodgers pass. Then Andrew got hot. He threw two touchdown passes and scampered for another. With 4:35 to play in the fourth quarter, we trailed 21–19 and had the ball first-and-10 on our 20-yard line.

To me, there is nothing better in football than when your quarterback develops a hot hand. It's like a golfer in the zone—the hot quarterback can make every throw in the book from every arm angle. That was what Andrew did in the second half, and really it marked the true beginning of the Luck era in Indianapolis.

But it wasn't easy. At one point in the second half Andrew got hit so hard that I thought he was dead. He fumbled the ball but somehow managed to recover it. As he lifted himself up he congratulated the Packer defensive lineman on the terrific hit. Typical Andrew. More typical: On the next play he completed a pass on third down to move the chains.

What did those two plays signify to me? For starters, that Andrew had the toughness to be an elite NFL quarterback. Remember, one of the reasons we picked Andrew over RG3 was because we thought Andrew, who is bigger than RG3, had a better chance at surviving in the NFL and would have a longer career. But it wasn't just his stature that led us to that conclusion; it was also his toughness. Imagine being in a violent car wreck every week, because that's often the level of beating an NFL quarterback takes week in and week out. And the thing is, the quarterback knows that the pain is coming, but he has to stand there in the pocket, keep his eyes downfield, and throw with accuracy—while expecting to get pulverized by 330-pound muscled maniacs whose ultimate motive in life is to rip your head off.

Andrew displayed immense courage on this two-play sequence. He also showed resiliency, which is another hallmark characteristic of the elite NFL quarterback. So often quarterbacks, especially the young ones, will develop a severe case of happy feet immediately after they've been driven into the turf by a defender. They basically tell themselves, *Screw this, I'm not getting hit again*, and then they'll take flight from the pocket at the first hint of danger. But not Andrew. The fact that he absorbed a monster hit on second down and completed a pass on third down to keep the drive alive revealed that he had the guts of a winner, that he was one helluva resilient NFL quarterback. The easy thing to do would have been for him to take off running or mail in the throw on that third-down play; instead, in that very difficult moment when he was in an ungodly amount of pain, he made a terrific throw.

On our final drive of the game, Andrew led us down the field, calmly completing short and intermediate passes. He was a surgeon out there, reading the Packer defense and dissecting it with pinpoint throws. He converted two third downs with passes to Reggie Wayne, and he scrambled for another third-down conversion.

With 35 seconds to play and the ball at the Green Bay four-yard line, Andrew found Reggie on the left side cutting in. Reggie caught the ball short of the end zone, but he dove and stretched over the goal line to score the touchdown. We won 30–27.

What a scene that was. Players fell to their knees and rolled on the turf after the final whistle blew. I hugged dozens and dozens of players, coaches, and fans. When I saw Jake, we grabbed each other again and we both started crying again. I told reporters then and I still believe it to this day: It was the greatest victory of my career, more important than even the two Super Bowls I was fortunate enough to win.

The locker room was unlike any I'd ever been in before. This wasn't just winning a game; it was our way of showing Chuck how much we cared for him, loved him. I told the players, "This is the greatest win in all my life. I've never been prouder of a group of guys than I am of you guys right now. Everybody was helping. Chuck was coaching his ass off up in the hospital for us. You know he was. We did it for him!"

Reggie Wayne then gave me a game ball—the first one I'd ever received in my life. But that wasn't the real game ball. After the game Jim Irsay drove down the street to the hospital to see Chuck. He gave him the actual game ball. I was still in the parking lot running the best tailgate party of my career.

The comeback win against the Packers propelled us for the rest of the season. Heading into our second-to-last game of the regular season against the Chiefs we were 9–5 and had a chance to clinch a playoff berth with a victory. Only one other team in NFL history had won 10 games in a season after losing 14 the year before—the 2008 Dolphins—and our success was directly tied to Andrew's rapid development, the players' commitment to one another, and their compassion for Chuck.

What made our charge to the playoffs even more unlikely was that we ended up placing thirteen guys on Injured Reserve. We'd have players come in off the street on Tuesday and play on Sunday. Sometimes I wouldn't even know their names. One game I saw our No. 97 sack the opposing QB. I had no idea who he was. I looked around the sideline and asked what his name was. "That's Jamaal Westerman, Coach," a player told me. Then when No. 97 got to the sideline, I walked over to him and said, "Yeah, way to go, Jamaal. Great job!"

We also had six rookies playing significant roles on offense, but we didn't allow our inexperience to hold us back. Our team became a reflection of Andrew—composed, confident, expecting to win. That's leadership. That's what great quarterbacks bring to a team.

In our next-to-last regular-season game we were tied with Kansas City at 13–13 midway through the fourth quarter. Then Andrew did it again. With time running out, he found Reggie Wayne in the back of the end zone on a third-down play for a seven-yard touchdown pass. We won 20–13, the sixth time in the season Andrew guided us to a victory in the fourth quarter after the game was tied or we were behind. We had punched our ticket to the postseason.

Andrew finished the game with 205 yards passing, and in the process broke Cam Newton's one-year-old record for most passing yards by a rookie quarterback (4,051). I was so proud of Andrew, and I told him so. But he genuinely didn't care about the record; he just wanted to know who I thought we'd be facing in the playoffs. This is another trait of the great QB: He doesn't linger in the joy of today; instead, he looks at what needs to be accomplished tomorrow.

On the Monday after the win in Kansas City we were back at work on Christmas Eve—and so was Chuck. He met with the players that morning and they gave him a rousing standing ovation. Chuck had a wide, wonderful smile on his face as he shook hands and hugged the players. I'll never forget that night walking to my car. I looked back over my shoulder and the light was off in Chuck's office. I sat in my car for five minutes and sobbed. We had done it. Our leader was with us again.

I honestly didn't give a crap about anything else that season; I just wanted to get Chuck healthy. On Wednesdays and Fridays, when Chuck was well enough, I'd drive to the hospital and visit with him after practice. We'd review notes and draw up plays for the next game. There were a few times he was in pretty bad shape, but his courage never wavered.

On the day after Christmas, Chuck was back on the practice field. I kept stealing glances over at him as he presided over the practice, and I could tell how much he was savoring being with the team again. When the thing you love most in your professional life is taken away, you realize you can't take anything for granted. Chuck had been coaching football for twenty-eight years, and now I could tell he was soaking in the little things that most of us in the profession lose sight of— most notably the camaraderie and the fellowship that are present on the best football teams.

With Chuck back on the sideline at Lucas Oil Stadium, we finished the regular season with a 28–16 win over the Texans. In the locker room Chuck was aglow. The players danced and hugged and chanted and then Chuck started bouncing up and down himself. You never would have thought that he had just spent three months undergoing leukemia treatment at the Indiana University Simon Cancer Center.

"This man is one hell of a fighter," Irsay said to the team in the locker room. "I wouldn't want to put the gloves on to fight him right now."

"I'm back here because of every man in here," Chuck told us. "My inspiration came week in and week out by watching you fight. You've given this city hope. . . . What you gave me was something that was better than the medicine the doctors could have given me."

To me, this was NFL football at its best.

The next week as we were preparing to face Baltimore in an AFC wild-card game I started feeling lightheaded on Thursday. I talked with our team doctor and I eventually went to the hospital that night. I had an inner-ear infection and the doctors thought it was messing with my blood pressure. I was released in time to fly with the team to Baltimore on Saturday. That night I felt fine.

But Sunday morning during our pregame meal I became extremely dizzy. As I was eating everything started spinning. *Oh shit, this isn't good*, I thought. The team doctor came over and said he needed to take me to the hospital, which was across the street from our hotel.

"No way I'm going to the hospital," I said. "No way. I'll call the game from the press box if I have to and not the sideline, but I'm not leaving the team."

The doctor then checked my eyes—they were fluttering—and he said, "You need to go to the hospital." It wasn't a request; it was a demand. I had never missed a practice or a game in my life before, but at some point it's necessary to follow the advice of your doctor. Chuck's recent cancer battle had taught me that.

So I checked in. In an examination room the doctors initially thought I was having a stroke. My blood pressure was 220 over 150. At this stage Jim Irsay called and asked me if Chris was with me. She wasn't; my wife was back in Indianapolis. "I'm sending a car with a driver to take her to the airport," Mr. Irsay told me. "A private plane will be waiting for her to bring her to you."

Chris was by my side two hours later.

Our offensive game plan was already in place. Our quarterback coach, Clyde Christensen, knew exactly what to do. Although I felt like a caged animal and desperately wanted to escape the hospital bed, I knew with Clyde calling the plays our offense was in capable hands.

The doctors let me watch the game, which didn't exactly help my blood pressure. We missed a couple of chances in the red zone for touchdowns, and that sealed our fate. We went down 24–9.

I was released from the hospital two days later. The doctors never figured out what had caused my blood pressure to spike. One guessed it was the inner-ear infection, and another thought it could have been a migraine headache, but no one was 100 percent certain. So what. At least I was alive.

Once I got home to Indianapolis I got a call from a reporter. He told me that I had been named the AP Coach of the Year, and that I was the first interim head coach ever to win the award. I nearly dropped the phone.

I was shocked.

I had hired an agent, Mike Brown, a few months earlier at the insistence of friends and family who encouraged me to "play the game." But I still wasn't going to change my ways. Never. You are always guaranteed to get the unvarnished, unplugged version of me.

And soon after word of winning AP Coach of the Year got out, the phone began to ring, ring, and ring. Another door was about to swing open.

You've got to love life in the NFL.

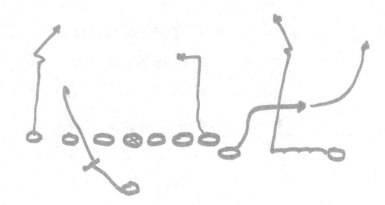

I sure as heck wouldn't want to be the third-stringer on one of Bruce's teams. Bruce will MF him to death. But I understand that he's really talking to me. He's coaching me through the third-stringer. It works for us, though I'm not sure how the third-stringer feels.

— CARSON PALMER

CHAPTER 9

CARSON PALMER

My day in Chicago went great.

At the end of the 2012 season, I was in our apartment in Indianapolis when my agent, Mike Brown, called to tell me that five teams were interested in having me interview for their head coach position. Only twelve months earlier I had been fired in Pittsburgh and believed my coaching career was finished. Life sure can be an up-and-down journey.

It was during my time of filling in for Chuck as the Colts' interim head coach that I finally decided to hire an agent. For years I had told everyone that I wasn't going to play politics. In retrospect, this probably hurt me. My wife certainly believes so.

"Bruce is incapable of kissing someone's butt," Chris says. "He doesn't give false praise to someone to get them to like him. For years he didn't want an agent doing that for him because he believed the results of his work should have spoken for him. But then Bruce got labeled in NFL circles as a 'career

201

coordinator.' He kept getting passed over to even interview for head coaching jobs while young guys who have hardly any experience somehow got labeled as 'future head coaches.' It made no sense."

Chris and Jake really got after me to finally get an agent midway through the 2012 season. We were having success and we kept hearing that I might have a chance to interview for a head coaching position at the end of the season. So I eventually called Mike Brown, who represented Clemson coach Dabo Swinney, and asked him to be my agent. Brownie, as we called him, was great. He immediately sprang into action.

"Bruce, we're going to get a résumé together and we're going to make this happen," he told me. "Just trust me."

After the season Brownie set up interviews with five teams that had head coaching vacancies. At first I was most intrigued with the Bears. I traveled to Chicago and met in Halas Hall with the team's general manager, Phil Emery. We talked for several hours as I detailed my plan of action for turning the team into a consistent winner. The most important thing, I stressed, was tailoring the offense to the strengths of quarterback Jay Cutler. Everything else builds on that foundation. I would have Jay pick exactly what he wanted to do—putting the accountability squarely on his shoulders—and then I would design an offense that would put him in a position to succeed.

I met with Jay and showed him my game plan and my call sheet. We went through several plays and broke them down together. He had a great arm and nice overall talent. Plus, he was a smart dude—a Vanderbilt man. You never know what a quarterback will do until you're in the heat of the battle with him, but just from the standpoint of arm talent, Jay had more than enough to flourish. He knew I loved the deep ball, and Jay could throw it out of the stadium.

I felt really good about how the day went in Chicago. In fact, I thought the discussions couldn't have gone any better. I also met with a few Bears front-office guys; Chairman George Halas McCaskey was great. I honestly figured I'd get the job.

But you never know in the NFL.

As I waited for the Chicago brass to make their decision, three of the five teams that had contacted my agent had already filled their head coach vacancies. Then the Bears decided to go with Marc Trestman, who lasted all of two seasons in the Windy City. I thought my shot at becoming an NFL head coach was over. The only team still interested was the Arizona Cardinals, but I was hesitant to interview for that job. The Cardinals had just fired my good friend Ken Whisenhunt, and I knew if I got the job I'd have to let go of all of his assistants, many of whom were close friends. Why would I have to fire them? Because a new head coach has to surround himself with his own guys. It only takes one discontented assistant to undermine an entire staff, and in the process that one guy can sabotage a season.

So I called Kenny. "Hey, man, I got a helluva dilemma," I said. "I didn't get the Bears job and the Cardinals now want me to come out and talk to them about replacing you. I don't feel comfortable coming to your city and firing all the guys you brought with you."

"No, B.A., you need to go and do the interview," he said. "You've earned this. Go for it."

The following day I flew out to Phoenix. That night I met with owner Michael Bidwill and general manager Steve Keim at Tarbell's, a Zagat Top Ten restaurant in the Valley.

I like to think of myself as a what-you-see-is-what-you-get kind of guy. So many people over the years have told me that I'm no good at playing politics and that I was a fool for never having a résumé on hand to give out to general managers. And maybe that did hurt me along the way; maybe I would have gotten a chance to interview for an NFL head coaching position when I was younger. But I've always felt it's important never to pretend to be something you're not. Maybe that's why I've gotten along so well with the majority of reporters over the years; I mean what I say and I say what I mean. With me, there is no sugarcoating, no dancing around the truth, no double talk.

I'm pretty sure I dropped my first F-bomb in the meeting with Michael and Steve only minutes into our conversation. "Where the fuck are our drinks?" I wondered aloud. Later, Michael would comment that his first impression of me was that I could use the word "fuck" as a noun, an adjective, and verb in a single sentence.

My loose mouth prompted a wry kinda shit-eating grin from Steve. The two of us are cut from the same blue-collar cloth. We're both hardcore Pennsylvania guys, we both had parents who worked factory jobs, and we've both been around the game our entire lives. Our rapport was lightning-flash instant. He told me he was looking for someone with experience. "Brother," I told him, "I've got a shitload of experience."

The next day we had a formal interview at the team facility in Tempe. I laid out my plan in detail and emphasized that we needed to bring in a veteran quarterback. "I'm not grooming a rookie," I said. "This team is built to win now and we don't have time to go through the growing pains we'll all suffer with a rookie quarterback."

I also explained that I needed to bring in my own coaches. I knew several in the organization wanted to keep Ray Horton as the defensive coordinator. I had nothing personal against Ray—we had worked together in Pittsburgh—but it was important for me to have the authority to hire my own guys. I already knew that I wanted Todd Bowles, who had played for me at Temple, to be my defensive coordinator.

I was particularly emphatic about hiring Todd. As I was pounding that home, Michael stood up and left the room. Man, I thought I had just talked myself out of the job, but the thing was, I only wanted it on those terms. When Michael got on the other side of the door I told Steve, "I told you before I came here that this was the deal."

"We'll work it out," Steve said.

About thirty minutes later Michael strolled back into the room and told me I was the new head coach of the Arizona Cardinals. I guess he needed to look himself in the mirror before deciding to hire an SOB like me.

I thanked everyone and then told Michael that I needed to call Jim Irsay. From an adjacent room I talked privately with Jim. He was ecstatic—I mean, as genuinely happy for me as my dad would have been had he been alive. Then I phoned Chris. She wasn't crazy about moving to the desert—"But it's a dry heat," I reminded her—and then she quickly realized that this would be the last job of my coaching career. She couldn't have been happier.

I went back into the meeting room and accepted the job. About five minutes later, Steve and I got to work. Our first task was obvious. "We've got to find a quarterback," I told him. "We need a QB the team will believe in and trust. If we can get this guy, I promise you we'll have a good team."

We immediately went after Drew Stanton, who was with me in Indy. He reminded me a lot of Kelly Holcomb—smart, tough, and full of grit. I really thought he was going to be our starter.

The morning after I was hired I picked up my cell phone and was astonished by the figures on the screen: I had 463 text messages and 295 missed calls. The majority, I recognized, were from coaches, and undoubtedly many were looking for a job.

I tried to return every text and every call. Even though I pretty much knew who I was going to hire to be my assistants, I wanted to pay my respects to the other coaches out there who were still wandering in the dark. So many times in my career that was me—unemployed in the offseason and unsure of what would come next. It nearly makes you want to lock yourself in your house, pull down the shades, and just sit in the dark, not because you feel sorry for yourself but because you don't know how you're going to support your family. You just don't know if a "next" phone call is going to come. The waiting—and the prospect of no job—can be excruciating.

Every January before the Super Bowl I always attended the Senior Bowl in Mobile, Alabama. Even when I didn't have a job, I would go and sit in the same hotel bar every night, talking to coaches and putting my name out there. At practice, I would take a lap around the field and talk to coaches and friends and let them know I would appreciate any help— break—they could give me.

When I went to Mobile as the Cardinals' head coach, I sat again in that very same seat at the bar and took the same lap around the field. I wanted all the guys to know that a lifetime assistant coach could make it. That's also why I returned those text messages and phone calls. I wanted to give guys hope that their next job was somewhere out there, even if it wasn't with me in Arizona.

I'll never forget the moment I became a fan of Carson Palmer's right arm.

The date was January 8, 2006, and the location was Paul Brown Stadium in Cincinnati. I was the Steelers' wide receivers coach and we were facing the Bengals and Carson in an AFC wild-card game.

I knew Carson was an extraordinary player. He had won the Heisman Trophy at USC in 2001 and earned the nickname "the Human Jugs Machine" because his passes are as fast and the spiral motion of his balls as perfect as those launched from the contraption of that name. A native of Orange County, he's 6'5", 230 pounds, and oozes California cool. When you see Carson you say to yourself, *Now that's what an NFL quarterback looks like.*

On Cincinnati's second offensive play of that playoff game, Carson called "999 Seam," meaning three receivers and the tight end were to run vertical patterns downfield. We were lined up in quarters coverage, meaning we had four defensive backs arrayed evenly across the field. At the line of scrimmage Carson saw our defensive alignment and made a snap decision: He would throw the ball to wide receiver Chris Henry, who Carson believed could outrun any cornerback in the league.

Carson took the snap at his own 12-yard line, dropped back seven steps, and fired the ball high into the gray wintry sky. Oh my God, it was a gorgeous throw. I was standing on the sideline as Henry ran right past me, and I remember looking up at the ball and thinking it may have been one of the most beautiful passes I had ever seen. It fell from the heavens and landed perfectly in Henry's arms. Carson hit him in stride. The ball traveled about 55 yards in the air and Henry added another 11 for a 66-yard gain.

I looked back at Carson and he was on the ground, writhing in pain. *Oh shit*, I thought. As he had released the ball, defensive end Kimo von Oelhoffen drove his shoulder into Carson's left leg. The hit tore Carson's anterior cruciate and medial collateral ligaments in his knee. Kimo said he heard two pops that sounded like gunshots. I know Kimo felt horrible about the injury. Hell, we all did. You never want guys on the opposing team to get hurt—never—and this looked like a devastating injury.

We ended up winning the game 31–17. But I wouldn't be telling the truth if I said Carson's injury didn't have an outcome in the final score. We captured the Vince Lombardi Trophy a month later. Still, I couldn't get Carson's pass out of my mind. I love the deep ball as much as anyone, and that throw by Carson was a masterpiece, an artistic beauty.

Carson worked his tail off to get ready for opening game of the following season. From afar, I admired his work ethic. Your quarterback needs to be the most driven player on your team—everyone else takes their cue from his actions—and it was clear to me that Carson had all the needed intangibles. For the next few years, as the Steelers and Bengals played twice a season, I always looked forward to being on the same field with the Human Jugs Machine, if for no other reason than to see him rifle spiraling pigskins into orbit.

Carson had a nice run in Cincinnati. After recovering from that knee injury that he suffered against us in the play-offs, he started all sixteen games in 2006 and only missed one offensive snap. That season he threw for over 4,000 yards for the first time in his career and was named MVP of the Pro Bowl. His work ethic was admired around the league.

The next season, 2007, he set a franchise record by throwing for 4,131 yards. He injured his elbow in 2008, but bounced back the following year to lead the Bengals to the playoffs. Carson was traded to the Raiders in 2011. His team didn't enjoy as much success certainly as Carson had hoped for—he went 8–16 as Oakland's starting quarterback over two seasons—but every time I saw him play I still marveled at that golden arm of his. What if he was my quarterback?, I often thought.

What if?

In January 2013, three weeks after I was named the Cardinals' head coach, Steve Keim walked into my office and asked me what I thought about Carson, who was then the starting quarterback for the Oakland Raiders. "We might be able to get him in a trade," Steve said.

"Well, what do we have to give up?" I asked.

"Not that much," Steve replied.

"If we get Carson," I said, "we will win right away. And every player on this team will know we are legit and we're gunning for the Super Bowl."

In early April 2013—four months after I was hired—we pulled the trigger on the trade. We sent a sixth-round pick to the Raiders (176th overall) in exchange for Carson and Oakland's seventh-round pick (219th overall). We also gave the Raiders a conditional seventh-rounder in the 2014 draft if Carson started thirteen games in the 2013 season.

Several NFL writers described the Cardinals as being in a "rebuilding phase" when I took over. I didn't believe that at all. *Not. One. Second.* For starters, I was too damn old to rebuild anything, and I wouldn't have taken the job if I thought it was going to take several years for us to become a Super Bowl contender. But I love it when writers dump on my team—and for the record, I have a great relationship with most NFL beat writers and I truly enjoy interacting with them—because that just gives us all the more motivation to work hard every day.

When we announced the trade at a press conference, I made it clear to reporters that the move was done for one reason: to win now. After examining our roster, I knew that the team was a quarterback away from contending for a championship. The Cardinals franchise hadn't been stable at the quarterback position since Kurt Warner retired after the 2009 season, and nothing will doom an NFL team's chances to rise to the top faster than being in flux at QB. We had already signed free agent quarterback Drew Stanton a month earlier, and now with Carson in the fold I felt we had a real shot to win our division and also make some noise in the postseason.

As soon as the deal was finalized, Carson flew to Phoenix. We sat down in my office and we talked for over an hour about everything except football—our shared love of golf, our wives, and our kids. I told Carson that one of the best days of my life was when my son, Jake, asked me to be the best man in his wedding. That act by Jake, I said, kind of validated everything I had done as a father. I wanted to let Carson into my heart, and the best way to do that was for me to talk about one of the greatest days of my life with Jake, who is my best friend, on par with Chris and Kristi.

That night Carson, owner Michael Bidwill, Steve Keim, and I went to dinner at a steakhouse called Mastro's City Hall in Scottsdale. The wine list is expansive at City Hall, and I learned that Carson is something of a wine connoisseur. We continued to hit it off, and I joked that we would be two cowboys riding off together into the sunset. "Let's make it a long ride," I told him, "a long and great ride."

Carson was different than any other NFL starting quarterback I had coached. He was mature, had kids, was an overall number one draft pick, and had been the face of two other franchises. Now he was entering the twilight of his career. This meant I had to handle him like no other QB I had been with. I couldn't be the cool uncle with Carson; I had to be more like an older brother, one who offered counsel more than edicts, and yet who would be bossy when needed.

Carson and I talked about how he best learns and relearns. He said he needed to take as many mental reps as possible during the week, meaning he liked to watch film of the upcoming opponent as early each week as possible. Most weeks we tried to have the game plan pop up on his tablet between 5 and 7 p.m. on Tuesdays. Some quarterbacks can look at a play once and commit it to memory then and there—Andrew Luck had that gift—but Carson likes to study each play over and over to make certain that he doesn't miss anything.

We usually have around 150 plays in the game plan. For each one, there is a formation to learn, a personnel group to learn, and the opponent's defensive tendencies to learn. Then Carson needs to know what to change each play to if he sees a certain look by the defense, and, if the change is to pass play, he must know who his first, second, and third receiver options are. It's a massive amount of both data and logic to absorb, catalog, and recall in seconds when needed. Think of cramming for your hardest college test, and you'll have some idea of the extent to which a starting QB in the NFL prepares week after week for each game. To help Carson get battle-ready we used cutting-edge technology.

At his home Carson could put on a virtual reality headset called STRIVR Oculus. Here's how it works: A 360-degree camera is mounted on a tripod and placed next to the quarterback at practice. The camera sees everything the quarterback sees as he faces the scout-team defense. So when Carson puts on the headset and moves his head in any direction he can see what is happening all around him at any moment in every part of the field. This is particularly useful for identifying the location of potential blitzes.

The technology also allows Carson to watch and evaluate his throwing mechanics. Most quarterbacks are like golfers; if their stroke is off, even in the most miniscule way, the ball simply won't hit its intended target. So Carson, in the comfort of his home, can study his arm angle and follow-through, his footwork, and his balance simultaneously when he throws. If he misses a pass in practice, he can quickly pinpoint the reason by examining the play from myriad perspectives.

I've been a fan of virtual reality for two decades. Back in the 1980s I told anyone who would listen that if someone could invent a headset to put on the quarterback that would allow him to visually take mental reps he'd be a millionaire. But it took until 2014 for it to be readily available. About fifteen NFL teams now use it.

You see yourself, you see your wide receivers, you see your running back behind you, and you see the multiplicity of defensive schemes that you face. Carson is addicted to it. He basically can practice at home without breaking a sweat. And our backup quarterbacks can get reps through VR. It's a wonderful tool.

Two days before games, Carson watches film to learn how pocket passers recently performed against our upcoming opponent. He wants to know where the defense was vulnerable and where were the danger zones that he should try to avoid. He also likes to view all the third-down plays of the team we're about to face. NFL games are won and lost on third downs, and Carson always looks to pick up tendencies that he could exploit.

On the day before games, Carson reviews our game plan in painstaking detail to discover one or two things he needs to work on before kickoff. Then we huddle together and I try to answer every question he has. Carson always wants more—more mental reps, more information about the defense, more time to study. All quarterbacks in the NFL work hard—they have to, or they won't be in the league for long—but Carson takes all that to another level.

This should be a lesson to all young football players who aspire to be a quarterback: Carson has as much arm talent as anyone, but it is his relentless off-the-field work that makes him a special NFL player.

In my first draft with the Cardinals we made a controversial selection in the third round when we picked safety Tyrann Mathieu out of LSU. He had been kicked out of school there—his core issue was a documented drug problem—but he had first-round talent.

When I met Ty before the draft I could tell he was a good kid. It absolutely crushed him to lose the thing he loved most in life: football. He politely asked me for an opportunity, and if I gave him one, he said he wouldn't disappoint me. I believed he was sincere.

Draft day came and we were able to pick Tyrann with the sixty-ninth overall selection. Since then Tyrann has been a model teammate and a great father, and now he's got a golden future.

There are too many times in the NFL when coaches and general managers are too worried about public opinion. We forget about the person and what the person is going through. The NFL is too quick to cast some players out of the league because they have a bad image. We're ruining lives.

Instead we need to try to fix the players. Is the problem alcohol? Drugs? Let's fix it. Let's try to address the problem rather than kick players to the curb because they have a tainted reputation. This is one of my biggest pet peeves with the NFL.

Another pet peeve—the insane work hours of NFL coaches.

After I was fired from Temple in 1988, I became the running backs coach for the Kansas City Chiefs. The head coach was Marty Schottenheimer and we worked unbelievable hours, typically staying in the office five days a week until one or two in the morning. Marty was a micromanager and he wanted to meet with his position coaches every day as a group. We'd sit in the office twiddling our thumbs watching the clock tick as we waited for Marty to come talk to us. It was aggravating as hell. I almost never got to see my kids before they went to bed.

That fall Jake started playing junior high football. His games were on Thursday evenings. But Thursdays were also when I usually broke down the film of our next game opponent the following week. So I was torn. I eventually walked into the office of Joe Pendry, our offensive coordinator, who I had known for years.

"Joe, man, I gotta see Jake play," I said.

"What do you mean?" Joe said.

"They are playing at the junior high right now," I said.

"Then go," he said.

"But you know Marty," I said. "He doesn't like anybody leaving the damn office before we meet with him for our OD [offense-defense] position meetings."

"I'll tell Marty you went jogging," Joe said. "When you come back, throw some water on your face so it looks like you've been sweating."

So every Thursday that fall I went to see Jake play and then I'd sprinkle water on my face before we met with Coach Schottenheimer. It was silly but necessary to keep my job. It was so important to see Jake play, to see his face light up when he spotted his old man sitting in the stands. The hassle was well worth it. I told myself then that if I ever became an NFL head coach, I would demand that my assistants carve family time into their schedules. Work will always be there; kids won't.

I missed so much of Jake's and Kristi's development because I was imprisoned in the office. One of the first rules I told my assistants in Arizona was that they had to be out of the office by 10 p.m. If they stayed later, then that was because they didn't want to go home. It's simply uncalled for to be sleeping in offices.

You know why? Because the game ain't that damn hard.

The first time I met with the Cardinal players I had a simple message: We have to trust each other.

"Everyone in the building has to trust that the other guys are doing their jobs," I said. "We have one cause, and that's to win the world championship. Every decision you make, on and off the field, is either going to help the cause or hurt it. You have to respect the cause—and respect each other. You have to respect the people cooking your food and cleaning the locker room because they are fighting for the cause as well."

I also emphasized that they had to respect the process of preparation.

"The process is what you do on Monday, Tuesday, Wednesday, Thursday, Friday, and Saturday," I said. "You can't think about Sunday on Monday. You gotta get Monday's work done, and only then can you move on to Tuesday. You can't have a bad practice on Wednesday, because you don't get a do-over. The process is key. No speech by me is going to get you ready to play. Snot bubbles and tears don't win shit. They'll get you knocked out real quick. If you respect the process, you'll be prepared, and there's never any pressure when you're prepared. I never feel any pressure calling plays, and I don't think you as players should feel pressure on Sundays when you step between the lines—as long as you've honored the process of preparation."

I told my players that I don't believe in "chemistry." That's the most overused word in football. Teams don't have chemistry, they have caring. When players and coaches truly care about each other they become accountable to each other. I've been in locker rooms where it's offensive guys versus defensive guys and where everyone is divided into cliques. It's the teams where all players are asking each other questions like, "Hey, how's the wife?" or "How are the kids?" that perform the best.

I laid down one law: We don't haze anybody on the Cardinals. There is no room for hazing on my team because we're going to need the young guys to win. I don't care if they carry helmets or water bottles—that stuff is easy—but there will be no demeaning hazing such as taping guys to the goalpost.

"Everyone needs to remember to help each other at all times," I told my players in our opening meeting. "And if a veteran sees a young guy who's partying too much, well, that veteran needs to get that young guy's ass out of the bar. Because if you don't, it will come back to bite all of us. That's what accountability is."

My first job with Carson was to figure out how to make him comfortable in our offense. We had talked about no-huddle, but whenever we ran it early in our first season together he looked a little out of sorts. His execution of the no-huddle was different than that of most of my other quarterbacks. He'd check with me on the sideline before running anything. Carson wanted to make sure we were in the right play rather than speed up the game. That often took time—precious time—but it became part of who we were.

I also knew I couldn't be too hard on Carson at practice. You can't publicly undress proven NFL players in practice. Carson has earned that. But that doesn't mean I can't get a point across by excoriating the backup quarterback about something—even though I'm really talking to Carson. To put it in no-mince words, you rip the third-stringer a new one so the starter gets the message.

Here's an example. We'll run two practices during training camp on two fields that are next to each other. If I see that the starter is making the same mistakes on his field as the backup is on his, I'll scream loud enough so everyone can hear. "What the fuck are you looking at?" I'll ask the backup. "It's cover three so you should be looking over here but you're looking over there. Your helmet is pointing that way so I know you're looking over there. And don't tell me you like the fucking matchup, because it wasn't man-to-man."

In cases like this, my words are aimed at the backup. But in reality, I'm trying to get my point across to the starter. And it's been my experience that the more colorful language I use—and if you didn't guess it, there aren't many four-letter words that *aren't* in my everyday vocabulary—the more successful I am in capturing the attention of my players.

I clearly got Carson's attention. In our first year together—his tenth season in the NFL—he threw for a career-best 4,274 yards. Carson and I simply clicked almost from the day we first met. I admired how hard he worked and how many hours he put in studying the game plan; defenses rarely surprised him. His arm was even better than I thought—he could wing it as good as any quarterback I'd ever been around—and he was a professional in every sense of the word, from how he interacted with teammates in the locker room to how he patiently dealt with the media to even signing every last autograph after every home game. Remember: the great quarterbacks still play the role of leader long after they walk off the field. The great ones earn the respect of their teammates as much with their actions outside the white lines as inside them. Carson is an example of this.

My Saturday night meetings with Carson were extremely productive in our first season together. He always came with great questions about certain plays that he was struggling to understand or execute. He was like the kid in school who always needed to be overprepared for the final exam—and I loved that about him.

"I wish I had thirty minutes a day with B.A., just so I could pick his brain," Carson says. "I know he can't do that because he's the head coach and he's got so many other responsibilities, but I really love the time I do get with him, because Bruce knows more about offensive football than anyone I've ever been around. He's seen it all and certainly thought about it all. A defense won't surprise him. It's comforting as a quarterback to know that your coach has all the answers."

My success with Carson continued into our second season together in Arizona, 2014, when he threw 11 touchdowns and only three interceptions in our first six games. His 95.6 passer rating was the second-highest of his career. His season ended early when he tore his ACL, but he helped us to an 11–5 record and a berth in the playoffs. And without his stellar play in those first six games, there is no way I win my second AP NFL Coach of the Year award in three seasons.

Then in 2015 Carson threw for another career-best 4,671 yards.

Yes, I think he does all right in our offense.

In 2014 our starters missed 160 games due to injury. Our roster was just ravaged. Carson went down. Our backup quarterback, Drew Stanton, went down. We were a M*A*S*H unit in red-and-white uniforms.

But that team still was able to win eleven games. Why? Because our players cared for each other and held themselves accountable to the team—our family—as a whole. We started every meeting by reading what we called an "Accountability Sheet." This listed all the mental errors and penalties committed during the previous practice.

Guys were terrified to have their names on that sheet. If a rookie or a relative newcomer made the list too often, a veteran player would straighten him out in the locker room. This isn't the coach's job; it's the job of the veterans to police the locker room and make sure everybody is mentally sharp every time we're on the practice field or in games. You can't create, much less tolerate, situations that pit players against players or players against coaches. If either occurs, you may as well throw in the towel on your season. But if you have strong veteran leadership and they are willing to keep guys in line, that can create an "us for us" dynamic in the locker room and on the field of battle. That environment is the one a head coach should try to build and sustain.

A head coach must have the trust of the veteran leaders on the team. If the veterans don't support their coach 100 percent, there is a danger of losing the locker room, losing the essence—the very foundation—of the meaning of "team."

I had only been the head coach of the Cardinals a few days when I reached out to defensive tackle Darnell Dockett. I didn't know Darnell, but I knew his story. He was the Cardinals' third-round draft pick in 2004 out of Florida State and quickly developed into one of the NFL's top defensive linemen. He was a three-time Pro Bowl player (2007, '09 and '10), and in September 2010 Arizona signed him to a six-year, $56 million contract extension. By the time I arrived in Arizona, Darnell had been a longtime locker room leader.

I knew I needed to speak to Darnell. I texted him, "Hey, hit me up. It's B.A. Give me a call. I want to talk to you ASAP."

Darnell, though, didn't recognize my number or my initials. I kept at it. The next time I texted him I wrote, "Hey, this is your coach. Give me a call. I want to check in with you."

Darnell had been in Ken Whisenhunt's doghouse—he had upset the former Cardinals staff by not allowing the Jets to score a late touchdown in a game, as the staff had ordered, because it was the only way for our offense to get the ball back—but none of that was my concern. I told Darnell to come to New Orleans during Super Bowl week. I suggested we meet at a bar for a cocktail. We did.

Sitting at a place just off the French Quarter, I explained to Darnell that I needed him to be a team leader and that his past problems with the old staff were just that—in the past. They didn't mean anything to me. I told him I'd give him a chance if he would give me a chance. We ended the night by toasting our new beginning. Darnell didn't drink, so I had one for him.

And just like that, Darnell and I had made a connection. I now knew one of our key defensive veteran leaders would have my back, and he knew I'd have his. The next thing I needed to do was convince the rest of the team that we could win right away.

When I meet with reporters at my daily press conference, I dress like I always do: a flat Kangol cap and a dress shirt with the top two buttons open. One of the players joked that I looked like I had just walked out of a 1970s nightclub, and didn't look anything like the typical NFL coach. That was a great compliment, because I didn't want to be the typical NFL head coach in any form or fashion.

I've always loved nice clothes. When I went to a Catholic high school we had to wear a jacket and a tie. But I didn't own a jacket. So my uncle gave me this really ugly plaid jacket. I wore that thing every day of my freshman year. All the other kids had like five different jackets in their wardrobe, but not me, because I didn't have the cash to buy a nice jacket. I absolutely dreaded putting on that ratty old plaid jacket every morning. But I did.

Until I got a job washing dishes at an Italian restaurant. The next year I had four suits and five different pairs of dress shoes. Every morning when I put on my new clothes I felt a sense of pride. I immediately began to love looking fresh and natty. You look good, you feel good.

I want my players to know that I have a little bit of swagger. Remember, my first real nickname was given to me back in York, Pennsylvania, by a black kid named Eddie Berry— "S.Q. Smooth." I've always had some flash, and wanted that kind of vibe to trickle down to my players. They needed to have an edge to them—just like I do—and I wanted them to play with the confidence that goes along with having swagger. I wanted that to become our identity, because my plan from day one was to create a culture where winning wasn't a goal; it was an expectation.

I never shy away from big expectations. As soon as I got the job I told anyone who would listen that this team had the talent to win a Super Bowl. I knew the Cardinals were coming off a 5–11 season, but after we acquired Carson, I believed we had the potential to do something out of the ordinary, to go the distance.

I told the players as much when I talked to them before training camp. "I've been with a lot of good teams," I said. "I have Super Bowl rings. This team has just as much talent as those teams. But this is your team. We won't win unless you decide you want to, unless you decide you're willing to make the sacrifices it takes to be great in this league."

Then I met individually with each player. I told each of them the same thing. "This is one of the most talented teams I've ever been a part of," I said to each of the players. "We *should* go to the playoffs. It's going to take work, but we can be special."

The difference between winning and losing in the NFL is paper thin. Every roster is populated with game-breaking players. But one of the key X factors in the sport is confidence. If a team truly believes in itself, man, that can be the winning touchdown on any given day. So I took it upon myself to try to pump up my players as much as I could.

We didn't win a Super Bowl in my first three years in Arizona, but we did get better each season—10–6 in 2013, 11–5 in 2014, and 13–3 in 2015.

I truly believed we would hoist the Vince Lombardi Trophy last season. But football, like life itself, doesn't always go as you draw it up.

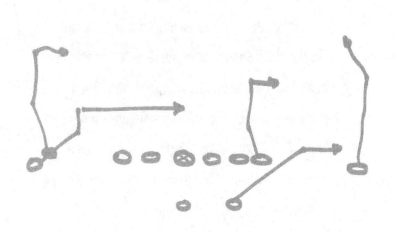

I'd venture to say that B.A. knows more about quarterbacking and play calling than any coach in the NFL. Good luck if you're a defensive coordinator and you want to surprise him. B.A. has the answer to every question the defense throws at him. And if you're his quarterback and you're struggling with something in your mechanics, B.A. will know exactly what the problem is and what needs to be done to solve it.

— CARSON PALMER

CHAPTER 10

THE FUTURE

If I was a college coach I'd run the no-huddle spread offense. I'd scour the country for the best athlete I could find and I'd line him up five yards behind center. I wouldn't necessarily call him my "quarterback." I'd probably refer to him as my "athlete playing quarterback."

At the high school level, athletes are so much easier to find than quarterbacks. Some high schools have full-field passing games, but not many do. Most just use half-field passing attacks, which means the quarterback only looks to one portion of the field in his reads. And if his first and second read options are covered, he'll just tuck it and run.

The rise of the spread offense in college football is decreasing the availability and hurting the development of potential NFL quarterbacks. The college spread quarterback gets the play call by looking at a sign that someone on the sideline holds up. He rarely uses a snap count—he just claps his hands or stomps his foot—and then he takes the snap in the shotgun position. He then chucks the ball about four yards downfield to a receiver slanting across the middle.

To me, that damn sure ain't what playing quarterback is all about. The most important trait needed to become a QB is leadership. But there is no leadership required of the quarterback in this version of the spread. He doesn't talk to his teammates in the huddle, he doesn't change the snap count—hell, he barely even reads the defense. The college spread quarterback doesn't learn the mental and physical skills needed to execute the intricacies of the NFL game. That puts the college spread QBs who aspire to play and succeed in the NFL at a distinct disadvantage.

The best college-level spread quarterback I've ever seen was Robert Griffin III. He was dynamite at Baylor, throwing for 37 touchdowns in 2011 on his way to winning the Heisman Trophy. But I didn't want to pick him when I was the offensive coordinator with the Colts the year we had the top pick in the draft. Why? Because I thought he didn't have a "feel" for the game—that he would struggle trying to run a traditional pro-style offense. Spread QBs don't have a sense of reading coverage and knowing where to go with their hot reads. They don't throw hot reads on sight adjustments in the spread, so they have to learn that. And they don't really read blitzes—they have one protection, which is slide right or slide left—and so that skill has to be taught as well.

If you draft a spread quarterback you can expect him to fail early in his career. That means he's going to need really great mental toughness to deal with this failure. He's definitely going to have to stay off social media, because no type of failure is accepted in that universe. Most rookie quarterbacks are going to suck anyway—it takes time and repetition to learn and adjust to the speed and the nuances of the NFL game—but he'll really be at a disadvantage if he's coming from a spread team and has no idea of the pro concepts.

I'm also always astonished at how NFL teams overreach for quarterbacks in the first round. But coaches are desperate, and for good reason: If you don't have a quality QB, your team probably won't be very competitive, which means you won't have a job for very long.

In my book, gazing twenty years into the future, I think the prototypical NFL quarterback will look a lot like today's Peyton, Ben, Carson, Andrew, and Tom Brady—guys who have heart and grit, big, strong, sturdy guys who have howitzers for arms and just enough athletic ability to scramble around in the pocket for an extra few seconds to allow their receivers to get open down the field. He'll have to be a leader, be smart as hell, and be the first guy in the building each morning and the last one to leave at day's end, just like all those guys.

Every so often there will be outliers like Russell Wilson at Seattle. Russell, who is 5'11", played in a pro-style offense at Wisconsin and is one of the smartest quarterbacks in the league. The Seahawk coaches have done a nice job devising a scheme for him that creates passing lanes. It's not easy for a quarterback to be six feet or under in the NFL—the only other short guy who has really lit it up in the last two decades has been the Saints' Drew Brees—but it can be done when the right player is with the right coaching staff.

* * *

I knew our 2016 season wasn't going to go as we'd hoped when we hosted the Seahawks on *Sunday Night Football* on October 23. After ending regulation play tied 3–3, we kicked a field goal on our opening drive of overtime. Then Seattle hit a field goal on its first offensive possession to knot the score 6–6.

We then moved down the field to set up Chandler Catanzaro for a game-winning 24-yard field goal attempt. Shit, I thought we had this one in the bag. The kick bonked off the left upright. The game ended 6–6.

I was so disappointed as I walked out of our home stadium that night. Our record fell to 3–3–1. Worse, we had had a chance to beat our division rival, and we didn't get it done. After the game I was feeling really low when I made it out to my car to begin my usual tailgate. That was when I saw Presley, my college-aged granddaughter. She smiled and gave me a hug—an embrace that reminded me of what's truly important in life. Presley is such a gifted young woman. She's a sports communication major in college, and it's so special to me to know that her grandfather's career has influenced what she wants to do with her life. Once again, even in the shadow of that tie, I won that tailgate.

But our season never really got on track after that tie to the Seahawks. I've got to do a better job at coaching in 2017. Carson and Larry Fitzgerald are coming back with me. The gunfighters are going to have at least one more shootout before we ride into the sunset.

We finished 2016 by winning our last two games, at Seattle (34–31) and at Los Angeles (44–6). The victory over the Seahawks was particularly important. Seattle has only lost five games at home in the last five years, and three of them have been to us. That gave us confidence heading into the offseason. We finished 4–1–1 in the division and the team that captured the NFC West—the Seahawks—never beat us.

Football is literally a game of inches and unpredictable bounces. We lost at least three games because of a bad snap, hold, or kick on special teams. The little things mean so much. I've got to do a better job with Carson in 2017. He played great in December but struggled early in the season because we practiced him too hard in August and September. His passes lost some velocity, which in turn caused him to lose some of his accuracy. But by midseason we learned to manage his practice reps—we limited his pitch count, so to speak—by resting him on Wednesdays and cutting the number of his throws in half on Thursdays. Again, by season's end he was playing at an extremely high level. In December he threw for 300 yards in every game except against the Rams—and we pulled him late in that contest because we had such a huge lead.

I talked to Carson at least once a week this past offseason, discussing his wife, his kids, and his golf game. He needed to decompress and get away from the game for a little while—this is good for all starting quarterbacks because it clears their minds—but now he's as dedicated as ever to win that first Super Bowl. I'm sixty-four and very aware the clock is ticking on my coaching career.

For a moment or two, in fact, I didn't know if I'd even make it back to the sideline in 2017.

* * *

The call came from the doctor on a Thursday night in December. I was on date night with Chris at a place called Steak 44. Our drinks had just arrived.

A few days earlier I had visited the doctor to get a hernia checked. But the ultrasound revealed more than the hernia issue. It showed a small spot on a kidney. The diagnosis was renal cell carcinoma. I had cancer again.

So I started 2017 with a different fight. My brother-in-law passed away from cancer of the esophagus in December. Shit, we had planned a wonderful golf trip together for this offseason and then, out of nowhere, he was told he had cancer and ten months later he was gone. He was going to bring his son on that golf trip, but my brother-in-law was too sick. I hate cancer.

The doctor removed a small portion of my cancerous kidney in February, and now I feel great. My energy has returned. I'm told I'm cancer free again. I'm ready for at least one more season of NFL football—maybe more.

I'm going to be missing a familiar face this season. A few days before I had my own cancer surgery in February I was at home at the lake house on a Saturday night when the phone rang. It was Mike Brown, my agent, and Brownie was calling just to check on me. He was fighting pancreatic cancer, but his doctors were optimistic about his chances for beating it. So on the phone we talked about the upcoming season, getting together in Indianapolis at the scouting combine like we usually did, and the golf tournaments that we were going to play in. He sounded great. Just full of life. Before hanging up, he wished me luck in my own surgery and reassured me that everything was going to be okay.

The next morning I received another call, this one from one of my assistants at the Cardinals, and the news literally brought me to my knees: Brownie was gone. He had died that night of an aneurysm. I told Chris and I hugged her so hard.

Brownie was responsible for helping us start our foundation, which promotes advocacy for kids in the foster care system, and he helped us raise money. Chris has become the driving force behind the foundation—"I practiced family law and could remember so many times when I was representing crazy parents and thinking, 'The person who needs a lawyer is the kid,'" Chris says—but Brownie was instrumental in making it happen. He could work a crowd at a fund-raiser like a seasoned politician, and his smile could light up a room like few others. He meant so much to Chris and me. Who knows? I may have never become an NFL head coach without him. Brownie will always be my one and only agent.

Between the death of my brother-in-law, losing Brownie, and my own battles with cancer, I now realize more than ever that nothing is guaranteed in life. Every day needs to be enjoyed and celebrated to the fullest. Roses need to be smelled, sunsets savored, time with family cherished. Moving forward, I want to be a beacon of hope for others struggling with cancer. My fight is their fight. I'm not coaching for myself in 2017; I'm coaching for everyone who's dealing with cancer. This is my charge.

Looking back on my life, I wouldn't change a thing. Well, maybe one thing.

I would have learned what a condom was when I was sixteen—but that's a story for another day.

* * *

At its core, coaching isn't about winning and losing. At the college level, coaching is about molding teenagers into men and leading them to become positive members of society. In the NFL, it's about building relationships.

Most NFL coaches don't socialize with their players. I do. When my players walk out of our stadium after Cardinals home games, the first car they'll see in the lot is mine. The trunk will be open and I'll be handing out beer, mixed drinks, shots—you name it. The bartender in me makes sure they're taken care of.

If a player had a bad game, I'm going to give him a beer and a big and sincere hug. If a player had a great game, I'm going to give him a beer and a big and sincere hug. You see, I know they each tried, they each gave it their best shot. Sometimes you come up short, sometimes you go over the top. If you've earned the trust of your teammates, if you've played with determination, if you've been a team player—regardless of a one-time outcome—you get the beer and the hug. And then I'm going to ask both players if there's anything I can do to help them get ready for the start of our preparation for the next game.

One time Larry Foote, after attending my tailgate, walked up to me. Larry has known me a long time—he played linebacker with me in Pittsburgh and Arizona and is now a Cardinals assistant—and he said, "B.A., how's it feel to be coolest coach in the NFL?"

I'd never thought of it that way. I told Larry, "Hey, I'm just being me, brother."

And a big part of me is rooted in the belief that you must take chances—in life and in football. If you don't try to take great shots down the field, you're never going to hit a great shot down the field. You gotta live smart—and never live scared.

I call plays and coach quarterbacks the same way: No risk it, no biscuit.

ACKNOWLEDGMENTS

I've loved one woman in my life. The sacrifices that Chris has made for me are too long to list here, but there's no question I wouldn't be where I am today without her. She makes me a better man. From the bottom of my heart, I thank you, Chris.

Our two children, Jake and Kristi, are my best friends. Growing up the son and daughter of a coach is extremely hard—the moving van always seemed to be pulling into our driveway—but I'm so proud of the adults they've become.

Lars Anderson is one of the best writers in America. He helped me turn a jumble of thoughts into what you now hold in your hands. But more important, Lars and I have become good buddies. I cherish our friendship and the long hours we've spent together. And thank you to Lars's wife, April, and their son, Lincoln, who is one cool little dude.

Mike Fetchko, the president of the agency ISM USA, is a longtime friend who I first met when I was the coach at Temple. Mike suggested the book idea to me seven years ago and he was instrumental in connecting me with Lars and Scott Waxman, who is Lars's literary agent.

Mauro DiPreta, the publisher of Hachette Books, championed this project and skillfully guided us to the finish line. David Lamb, an assistant editor at the imprint, showed a keen eye for detail and made sure our deadlines were met. And Joanna Pinsker, our publicist at Hachette Books, worked diligently to promote *The Quarterback Whisperer.*

Finally, I'd like to thank all the players I've had the honor of coaching over the years. My success is your success. I'm so grateful for the many relationships I've forged over the course of my coaching career—especially with my quarterbacks.

ABOUT THE AUTHORS

BRUCE ARIANS is currently the head coach of the NFC powerhouse the Arizona Cardinals. In three years he has taken the team from last place in their division to the NFC Championship. He has also guided quarterback Carson Palmer to the best results of his long career. He has twice been named the NFL's Head Coach of the Year.

LARS ANDERSON is the bestselling author of six books including *Carlisle vs. Army* and *The Storm and the Tide*. He is a senior writer at Bleacher Report.